Mastering Data Science Using R Programming

Unleashing Insights with R

Mastering Data Science Using R Programming

Unleashing Insights with R

Venkataramana Battula

A. V. Krishna Prasad

Maturi Venkata Subba Rao (MVSR) Engineering College,
Hyderabad, India

BSP **BS Publications**

An Imprint of **BSP Books Pvt. Ltd.**
4-4-309/316, Giriraj Lane,
Sultan Bazar, Hyderabad - 500 095

Mastering Data Science Using R Programming: Unleashing Insights with R
***by* Venkataramana Batula and A. V. Krishna Prasad**

Published by:

BSP **BS Publications**
An Imprint of **BSP Books Pvt. Ltd.**
4-4-309/316, Giriraj Lane, Sultan Bazar,
Hyderabad – 500 095.
Phone: 040 – 23445688
e-mail: info@bspbooks.net
www.bspbooks.net

ISBN: 978-93-48734-53-2 (Hardback)

Dedicated to the tireless students, the supportive colleagues, and the unwavering love of family members and friends. Your encouragement and inspiration fuel the pages of this textbook.

Preface

Introducing our Data Science textbook!

Whether you're a student diving into the field or a professional looking to enhance your skills, this guide is tailored to suit your needs. Organized into seven units, each delves into a distinct facet of data science. We kick off with the foundational principles in **Data Science** Fundamentals, examining essentials such as Linear Algebra and Eigen values. Statistical Modeling follows, introducing concepts like Random Variables and Hypothesis Testing. Then, we delve into Predictive Modeling, where Linear Regression and Logistic Regression take center stage. Moving forward, **R Programming** covers a spectrum from Variables and Functions to Control Structures and Simulation, providing a comprehensive understanding of this vital tool.

In Classification and Clustering, you'll delve into Performance Measures and the K-Means Algorithm. Then, we move on to Association Rule Mining and Case Studies, offering practical insights into real-world applications.

Throughout the book, we aim to provide clear explanations and relevant examples to help you understand and apply these concepts effectively. Each unit builds upon the previous one, ensuring a cohesive learning journey. We hope this textbook serves as a valuable resource in your quest to master Data Science.

Happy learning!

Contents

Chapter 1

Introduction to Data Science

Data science is a multidisciplinary field that involves using various statistical, mathematical, and computational techniques to extract insights and knowledge from data. Data science encompasses a broad range of techniques, including data visualization, data mining, machine learning, and statistical analysis. The ultimate goal of data science is to use these techniques to make informed decisions and predictions. The data used in data science can come from a variety of sources, including social media, websites, sensors, and other digital devices. This data is often unstructured and requires cleaning and preprocessing before it can be analyzed. Once the data is prepared, it can be analyzed using statistical methods to identify patterns, relationships, and trends. One of the key aspects of data science is machine learning, which involves using algorithms to identify patterns in data and make predictions based on those patterns. Machine learning can be used for a variety of tasks, including image recognition, natural language processing, and fraud detection. Data science also involves data visualization, which is the process of creating visual representations of data to help identify patterns and trends. Visualization tools can be used to create charts, graphs, and other visualizations that make it easier to understand complex data sets.

Defining Data Science

Data Science is the systematic study of vast volumes of data to uncover patterns, trends, and insights that can inform decision-making processes across various domains. In essence, it's the art and science of transforming raw data into actionable knowledge. This interdisciplinary field encompasses a range of techniques and methodologies from statistics, computer science, mathematics, and domain expertise to extract meaningful information from data.

The Role of Data Science

At its core, Data Science revolves around collecting, processing, analyzing, and interpreting data to extract valuable insights. It involves a combination of statistical analysis, machine learning algorithms, data visualization techniques, and domain knowledge to make sense of complex datasets. By leveraging advanced computational tools and techniques, Data Scientists can uncover hidden patterns and correlations that can drive business strategies, scientific discoveries, and societal advancements.

Where is Data Science Needed?

1. **Business and Finance**: In the realm of business and finance, data science is indispensable for market analysis, risk assessment, fraud detection, and customer segmentation. By analyzing consumer behavior and financial trends, organizations can optimize pricing strategies, mitigate risks, and identify lucrative investment opportunities.

2. **Healthcare and Medicine**: Data science is revolutionizing healthcare by enabling predictive modeling, personalized medicine, and disease diagnosis. By analyzing electronic health records, genomic data, and medical imaging, healthcare providers can improve patient outcomes, optimize treatment protocols, and identify potential health risks at an early stage.

3. **Retail and E-Commerce**: Retailers leverage data science to enhance customer experiences, optimize inventory management, and personalize marketing campaigns. By analyzing purchase history, browsing patterns, and demographic information, retailers can tailor their offerings to meet the evolving needs and preferences of consumers.

4. **Transportation and Logistics**: Data science is reshaping the transportation and logistics industries by optimizing route planning, predicting demand, and minimizing operational costs. By analyzing traffic patterns, weather conditions, and delivery routes, companies can streamline supply chain operations and enhance the efficiency of transportation networks.

5. **Education and Research**: In the field of education and research, data science facilitates data-driven decision-making, student performance analysis, and academic research. By analyzing educational data, institutions can identify areas for improvement, personalize learning experiences, and enhance student outcomes.

6. **Energy and Utilities**: Data Science is playing a vital role in the energy and utilities sector by optimizing resource

1.1 Linear Algebra for data science

Linear Algebra is a fundamental branch of mathematics that plays a critical role in data science. It provides the tools necessary for representing and manipulating data in a structured and efficient way. Here are some of the key concepts of linear algebra that are essential for data science:

- **Vectors and Matrices:** Vectors are a set of numbers arranged in a specific order, while matrices are an array of numbers arranged in rows and columns. Vectors and matrices are used to represent data in a structured format.

- **Matrix Operations:** Matrix operations include addition, subtraction, multiplication, and inversion. These operations are used extensively in data science for tasks such as regression, classification, and clustering.

- **Linear Transformations:** Linear transformations involve transforming vectors and matrices by multiplying them with a transformation matrix. These transformations are used in data science for tasks such as image processing and feature extraction.

- **Eigenvectors and Eigenvalues:** Eigenvectors and eigenvalues are used to represent the properties of linear transformations. They are used in data science for tasks such as dimensionality reduction and principal component analysis.

- **Singular Value Decomposition (SVD):** SVD is a technique used to decompose a matrix into its constituent parts. It is used in data science for tasks such as image compression and data clustering.

1.2 Linear Equations

Linear equations play an important role in data science, as many real-world phenomena can be modeled using linear equations. In particular, linear regression is a commonly used technique in data science that involves fitting a linear equation to a dataset to describe the relationship between the input variables and the output variable.

Linear regression can be used for various tasks, including predicting housing prices, stock prices, and customer behavior. The linear equation used in linear regression can be represented as follows:

$$y = b_0 + b_1x_1 + b_2x_2 + ... + b_nx_n$$

where y is the output variable, $x_1, x_2, ..., x_n$ are the input variables, b_0 is the intercept, and $b_1, b_2, ..., b_n$ are the coefficients that determine the relationship between the input variables and the output variable.

To fit a linear regression model to a dataset, the coefficients $b_0, b_1, b_2, ..., b_n$ are estimated using a method called least squares. Least squares involves finding the values of the coefficients that minimize the sum of the squared differences between the predicted values and the actual values in the dataset.

Linear equations can also be used for other tasks in data science, such as optimization and constraint satisfaction. For example, linear programming is a technique used to optimize a linear objective function subject to linear constraints. Linear equations are used to represent the objective function and the constraints in this technique.

1.3 Distance

Distance measures in data science are algorithms that quantify the similarity or dissimilarity between two or more objects. These algorithms find common use across various data science applications like clustering, classification and recommendation systems.

Choosing the right distance measure is crucial for optimizing the performance of a data science model. It's essential to thoughtfully evaluate which distance measure best suits a specific problem, as the effectiveness of different distance measures varies depending on the data's characteristics.

Table 1.1: Common Distance Measures

Distance Measure	**Formula**
Euclidean Distance	$d(\mathbf{p},\mathbf{q}) = \sqrt{\sum_{i=1}^{n}(q_i - p_i)^2}$
Manhattan Distance	$d(\mathbf{p},\mathbf{q}) = \sum_{i=1}^{n} \lvert q_i - p_i \rvert$
Chebyshev Distance	$d(\mathbf{p},\mathbf{q}) = \max_i \lvert q_i - p_i \rvert$
Minkowski Distance	$d(\mathbf{p},\mathbf{q}) = (\sum_{i=1}^{n} \lvert q_i - p_i \rvert^p)^{\frac{1}{p}}$
Cosine Similarity	$\text{similarity}(\mathbf{p},\mathbf{q}) = \frac{\mathbf{p}\cdot\mathbf{q}}{\lVert\mathbf{p}\rVert\lVert\mathbf{q}\rVert}$
Jaccard Distance	$d(\mathbf{p},\mathbf{q}) = 1 - \frac{\lvert\mathbf{p}\cap\mathbf{q}\rvert}{\lvert\mathbf{p}\cup\mathbf{q}\rvert}$
Hamming Distance	$d(\mathbf{p},\mathbf{q}) = \sum_{i=1}^{n}(p_i \neq q_i)$

Applications of Distance Measures
Distance measures are used in various applications in data science:

- **Clustering:** Distance measures help in grouping similar data points together.
- **Classification:** They assist in assigning labels or categories to data points based on their similarity.
- **Anomaly Detection:** Distance measures aid in identifying unusual or outlier data points.
- **Recommendation Systems:** They are used to recommend items or content similar to what the user has interacted with.
- **Dimensionality Reduction:** Techniques such as t-SNE and PCA use distance measures to map high-dimensional data into a lower-dimensional space while preserving distances.

When selecting distance measures, several factors should be considered:

- **Nature of Data:** The type of data being analyzed influences the choice of distance measure.
- **Scale and Units:** The scale and units of the data may require standardization or normalization.
- **Dimensionality:** Some distance measures perform better in high-dimensional spaces.
- **Computational Complexity:** The efficiency of the distance measure in large datasets is important.

1.4 Hyperplane

A hyperplane is a flat affine subspace of dimension $p-1$ in an p-dimensional space. The equation of a hyperplane in p-dimensional space can be represented as:

$$\beta_0 + \beta_1 x_1 + \beta_2 x_2 + \ldots + \beta_p x_p = 0$$

Where:

- $\beta_0, \beta_1, \beta_2, \ldots, \beta_p$ are the coefficients of the hyperplane.
- $x_1, x_2, \ldots, x_p$ are the features of the data points.

A hyperplane is a fundamental concept in geometry and linear algebra. It represents a flat subspace of one less dimension than its surrounding space. In data science, hyperplanes are extensively used in support vector machines (SVMs) for binary classification.

Example: In a 2-dimensional space, a hyperplane is a line separating data points of different classes. SVMs aim to find the optimal hyperplane that maximizes the margin between the classes.

Subspace A subspace is a subset of a vector space that satisfies the properties of a vector space itself. It includes the zero vector and is closed under addition and scalar multiplication. In data science, subspaces are often encountered in dimensionality reduction techniques like principal component analysis (PCA).

Example: PCA identifies principal components (subspaces) that capture the most variance in the data, forming a lower-dimensional subspace while retaining essential information.

Halfspace A halfspace is a region of space bounded by a hyperplane. The equation of a halfspace is represented as:

$$\beta_0 + \beta_1 x_1 + \beta_2 x_2 + \ldots + \beta_p x_p \geq 0$$

or

$$\beta_0 + \beta_1 x_1 + \beta_2 x_2 + \ldots + \beta_p x_p \leq 0$$

depending on which side of the hyperplane defines the halfspace.

A halfspace is a region of space divided by a hyperplane into two parts: the positive and negative halfspaces. In data science, halfspaces are integral to linear classifiers such as perceptrons and logistic regression.

Example: In a binary classification problem, a halfspace represents a linear boundary dividing the feature space into regions corresponding to different classes.

1.5 Eigen Values

Eigenvalues and eigenvectors are important concepts in linear algebra that are widely used in data science, particularly in the context of dimensionality reduction techniques such as principal component analysis (PCA), linear discriminant analysis (LDA), and singular value decomposition (SVD). Eigenvalues and eigenvectors are closely related to linear transformations. Given a linear transformation, an eigenvector is a vector that, when transformed by the transformation, is scaled by a scalar value known as the eigenvalue. In other words, the eigenvector retains its direction but is scaled by a certain factor.

1.6 Eigen Vectors

In PCA, the goal is to reduce the dimensionality of a high-dimensional dataset while retaining as much information as possible. The technique involves finding the principal components of the dataset, which are the eigenvectors of the covariance matrix of the data. The eigenvalues of the covariance matrix indicate the variance of the data along each principal component, and the principal components with the highest eigenvalues capture the most variance in the data. In LDA, the goal is to find a linear transformation that maximizes the separation between different classes of data points. The technique involves finding the eigenvectors of the scatter matrix, which is a measure of the spread of the data within and between classes. The eigenvectors with the highest eigenvalues indicate the directions that maximize the separation between the classes. In SVD, the goal is to decompose a matrix into its singular values, which are equivalent to the eigenvalues of the matrix's covariance matrix, and its singular vectors, which are equivalent to the eigenvectors of the matrix's covariance matrix. SVD is commonly used in data science for various tasks, such as image processing, recommendation systems, and natural language processing.

PCA: Step-by-Step Example

Step 1: Data Normalization

First, we center the data by subtracting the mean of each feature from the respective feature values.

Compute the mean of Feature 1:

$$\bar{x}_1 = \frac{2+3+4}{3} = 3$$

Compute the mean of Feature 2:

$$\bar{x}_2 = \frac{3+4+5}{3} = 4$$

Subtract the means from the original data:

Feature 1	Feature 2
-1	-1
0	0
1	1

Step 2: Compute the Covariance Matrix

Next, we calculate the covariance matrix of the centered data.

The covariance matrix Σ is given by:

$$\Sigma = \frac{1}{n}\sum_{i=1}^{n}(\mathbf{x}_i - \bar{\mathbf{x}})(\mathbf{x}_i - \bar{\mathbf{x}})^T$$

Where n is the number of data points, $\mathbf{x}_i$ is the i-th data point, and $\bar{\mathbf{x}}$ is the mean vector.

In our case, $n = 3$.

The covariance matrix for our centered data:

$$\Sigma = \frac{1}{3}\left(\begin{bmatrix}-1\\0\\1\end{bmatrix}\begin{bmatrix}-1 & 0 & 1\end{bmatrix}\right) = \frac{1}{3}\begin{bmatrix}1 & 0 & -1\\0 & 0 & 0\\-1 & 0 & 1\end{bmatrix}$$

Step 3: Compute Eigenvalues and Eigenvectors

Next, we find the eigenvalues (λ) and eigenvectors ($\mathbf{v}$) of the covariance matrix Σ.

Using the characteristic equation $\Sigma\mathbf{v} = \lambda\mathbf{v}$, we solve for λ and $\mathbf{v}$.

Step 4: Sort Eigenvalues

Sort the eigenvalues in decreasing order and their corresponding eigenvectors.

Step 5: Choose Principal Components

Choose the top k eigenvectors based on the explained variance you want to retain.

Step 6: Project Data onto Principal Components

Project the centered data onto the chosen principal components.

Compute Eigenvalues and Eigenvectors

Given the covariance matrix:

$$\Sigma = \frac{1}{3}\begin{bmatrix} 1 & 0 & -1 \\ 0 & 0 & 0 \\ -1 & 0 & 1 \end{bmatrix}$$

Step 1: Eigenvalue Equation

The eigenvalue equation is $\Sigma \mathbf{v} = \lambda \mathbf{v}$, where λ is the eigenvalue and $\mathbf{v}$ is the corresponding eigenvector.

Step 2: Solve the Characteristic Equation

We need to solve the characteristic equation $|\Sigma - \lambda I| = 0$, where I is the identity matrix.

Subtract λ from the diagonal of Σ:

$$\begin{vmatrix} 1-\lambda & 0 & -1 \\ 0 & -\lambda & 0 \\ -1 & 0 & 1-\lambda \end{vmatrix} = 0$$

Step 3: Solve the Equation

Solve the determinant equation to find the eigenvalues λ.

$$(1-\lambda)((-\lambda)(1-\lambda)) - 0 - (-1)(0) = 0$$

$$(1-\lambda)(\lambda^2 - \lambda) = 0$$

$$\lambda^3 - 2\lambda^2 + \lambda = 0$$

This gives us a cubic equation. We need to find the roots of this equation.

Step 4: Find Eigenvalues

We can factor out λ and solve the quadratic equation:

$$\lambda(\lambda^2 - 2\lambda + 1) = 0$$

$$\lambda(\lambda - 1)^2 = 0$$

This equation gives us eigenvalues $\lambda_1 = 0$ and $\lambda_2 = 1$.

Step 5: Compute Eigenvectors

For $\lambda_1 = 0$:

$$\Sigma - 0I = \begin{bmatrix} 1 & 0 & -1 \\ 0 & 0 & 0 \\ -1 & 0 & 1 \end{bmatrix}$$

Perform Gaussian elimination to find the null space. We find the eigenvector corresponding to $\lambda_1 = 0$ is:

$$\mathbf{v}_1 = \begin{bmatrix} 1 \\ 0 \\ 1 \end{bmatrix}$$

For $\lambda_2 = 1$:

$$\Sigma - 1I = \begin{bmatrix} 0 & 0 & -1 \\ 0 & -1 & 0 \\ -1 & 0 & 0 \end{bmatrix}$$

Perform Gaussian elimination to find the null space. We find the eigenvector corresponding to $\lambda_2 = 1$ is:

$$\mathbf{v}_2 = \begin{bmatrix} -1 \\ 0 \\ 1 \end{bmatrix}$$

Now, we have computed the eigenvalues and eigenvectors for the covariance matrix Σ.

Step 6: Sort Eigenvalues

Sort the eigenvalues in descending order.

For our example, the eigenvalues are $\lambda_1 = 1$ and $\lambda_2 = 0$. Thus, after sorting, the eigenvalues are:

$$\lambda_1 = 1$$

$$\lambda_2 = 0$$

Step 7: Choose Principal Components

After computing the eigenvalues and eigenvectors, we choose the principal components based on the explained variance or the proportion of total variance they capture. Typically, we select the top k eigenvectors corresponding to the largest eigenvalues, as they explain the most variance in the data.

Linear Discriminant Analysis (LDA) Example

Step 1: Data Preparation

Given:

- Class 1:
  - Feature 1: $[1, 2, 2]$
  - Feature 2: $[1, 3, 2]$
- Class 2:
  - Feature 1: $[4, 5, 6]$
  - Feature 2: $[5, 7, 6]$

Step 2: Compute the Mean Vectors for Each Class
For Class 1:

$$\bar{x}_1 = \frac{1+2+2}{3} = \frac{5}{3},$$
$$\bar{x}_2 = \frac{1+3+2}{3} = 2$$

For Class 2:

$$\bar{y}_1 = \frac{4+5+6}{3} = 5,$$
$$\bar{y}_2 = \frac{5+7+6}{3} = 6$$

Step 3: Compute the Scatter Within Classes (S_W)

For Class 1:

$$S_{w1} = \begin{bmatrix} \frac{4}{9} & -\frac{1}{3} \\ -\frac{1}{3} & 1 \end{bmatrix}$$

For Class 2:

$$S_{w2} = \begin{bmatrix} 1 & -1 \\ -1 & 1 \end{bmatrix}$$

Thus, $S_w = \begin{bmatrix} \frac{13}{9} & -\frac{4}{3} \\ -\frac{4}{3} & 2 \end{bmatrix}$

Step 4: Compute the Scatter Between Classes (S_b)

$$S_b = \begin{bmatrix} \frac{100}{9} & \frac{40}{3} \\ \frac{40}{3} & 16 \end{bmatrix}$$

Compute the Eigenvalues and Eigenvectors
Given $S_w^{-1} S_b$, we compute its eigenvalues and eigenvectors.
Recall:

- S_w is the within-class scatter matrix.
- S_b is the between-class scatter matrix.

We need to solve the generalized eigenvalue problem:

$$S_w^{-1} S_b v = \lambda v$$

Where:

- v is the eigenvector.
- λ is the eigenvalue.

For this problem, we already calculated S_w and S_b.
From previous calculations, we have:

$$S_w = \begin{bmatrix} \frac{13}{9} & -\frac{4}{3} \\ -\frac{4}{3} & 2 \end{bmatrix}$$

$$S_b = \begin{bmatrix} \frac{100}{9} & \frac{40}{3} \\ \frac{40}{3} & 16 \end{bmatrix}$$

We compute S_w^{-1} first. Inverse of S_w is:

$$S_w^{-1} = \frac{1}{|S_w|} \cdot \text{adj}(S_w)$$

Where $|S_w|$ is the determinant of S_w and $\text{adj}(S_w)$ is the adjugate (or adjoint) of S_w.

For 2×2 matrix S_w:

$$|S_w| = \left(\frac{13}{9} \times 2\right) - \left(-\frac{4}{3} \times -\frac{4}{3}\right) = \frac{26}{9} - \frac{16}{9} = \frac{10}{9}$$

The adjugate of S_w is obtained by swapping the elements on the main diagonal and changing the sign of the off-diagonal elements:

$$\text{adj}(S_w) = \begin{bmatrix} 2 & \frac{4}{3} \\ \frac{4}{3} & \frac{13}{9} \end{bmatrix}$$

Thus,

$$S_w^{-1} = \frac{9}{10} \begin{bmatrix} 2 & \frac{4}{3} \\ \frac{4}{3} & \frac{13}{9} \end{bmatrix} = \begin{bmatrix} \frac{9}{5} & \frac{12}{10} \\ \frac{12}{10} & \frac{117}{90} \end{bmatrix}$$

Now, we compute $S_w^{-1} S_b$:

$$S_w^{-1} S_b = \begin{bmatrix} \frac{9}{5} & \frac{12}{10} \\ \frac{12}{10} & \frac{117}{90} \end{bmatrix} \cdot \begin{bmatrix} \frac{100}{9} & \frac{40}{3} \\ \frac{40}{3} & 16 \end{bmatrix}$$

Please perform the multiplication and subsequent calculations in order to obtain the eigenvalues and eigenvectors.

Choose Discriminants Choose the discriminants based on the eigenvalues. If there are k classes, then the number of discriminants is $k - 1$.

Project the Data Project the data onto the discriminants to get the transformed dataset.

1.7 Exercises

1.7.1 Short and Long Answer Questions

1. Define the concept of data science and its significance in modern industries.

2. List the fundamental principles of linear algebra relevant to data science.
3. Explain the concept of eigenvalues and eigenvectors in the context of linear algebra for data science.
4. Discuss the importance of hyperplanes and half spaces in machine learning algorithms.
5. Given a set of linear equations, solve them using appropriate linear algebra techniques.
6. Apply the concepts of distance metrics to measure similarity between data points.
7. Analyze a dataset and determine the eigenvalues and eigenvectors using appropriate computational methods.
8. Compare and contrast different methods for solving linear equations in data science applications.
9. Evaluate the effectiveness of various distance metrics in capturing the similarity between high-dimensional data points.
10. Assess the significance of linear algebra concepts such as hyperplanes and half spaces in machine learning algorithms.

1.7.2 Fill in the Blanks

1. Linear algebra is essential for data science, especially in tasks like ______.
2. Eigenvalues are often used to understand how much ______ a transformation applies to its corresponding eigenvector.
3. In linear algebra, a ______ is a set of vectors that are linearly independent and span the vector space.
4. The m______ of a matrix determines whether it can be inverted or not.
5. Half spaces are regions of space that lie on one side of a ______.
6. In data science, linear equations are used to model relationships between ______.
7. The dot product of two vectors yields a ______, not another vector.
8. Distance between two points in Euclidean space can be computed using the ______.
9. Singular Value Decomposition (SVD) decomposes a matrix into ______.
10. In linear algebra, eigenvectors represent directions in space that are only scaled by a ______.

1.7.3 Multiple Choice Questions

1. What is data science?
   A) The study of computers
   B) The study of collecting and analyzing data to gain insights
   C) The study of rocket science
   D) The study of plants

2. Which branch of mathematics is essential for data science?
   A) Calculus
   B) Trigonometry
   C) Linear Algebra
   D) Geometry

3. What are linear equations used for in data science?
   A) To solve complex algorithms
   B) To model relationships between variables
   C) To draw graphs
   D) To create pie charts

4. What is a hyperplane in linear algebra?
   A) A plane with no dimensions
   B) A plane that divides a space into two half-spaces
   C) A plane in 3-dimensional space
   D) A plane with curved edges

5. What term describes the region of space on one side of a hyperplane?
   A) Quarter space
   B) Full space
   C) Half space
   D) Hyper space

6. What are eigenvalues used for in linear algebra?
   A) They represent the magnitude of eigenvectors
   B) They define the direction of eigenvectors
   C) They measure the size of matrices
   D) They solve linear equations

7. What are eigenvectors?
   A) Vectors that don't change direction when a linear transformation is applied
   B) Vectors with varying magnitudes
   C) Vectors with constant magnitudes
   D) Vectors that change direction when a linear transformation is applied

8. How is distance computed between two points in Euclidean space?
   A) Using the Manhattan distance
   B) Using the Pythagorean theorem
   C) Using the cosine similarity
   D) Using the dot product

9. Which matrix operation involves finding the transpose of a matrix?
   A) Addition
   B) Multiplication
   C) Transposition
   D) Inversion

10. In linear algebra, what does the rank of a matrix represent?
    A) The number of rows in the matrix
    B) The number of columns in the matrix
    C) The number of non-zero rows after row reduction
    D) The number of non-zero elements in the matrix

11. What is the determinant of a matrix used for?
    A) Finding the sum of elements in a matrix
    B) Determining if a matrix is invertible
    C) Finding the product of elements in a matrix
    D) Determining the shape of a matrix

12. Which of the following is not a type of matrix?
    A) Identity matrix
    B) Square matrix
    C) Rectangular matrix
    D) Scalar matrix

13. What is the main objective of Principal Component Analysis (PCA)?
    A) To reduce the dimensionality of data
    B) To increase the complexity of data
    C) To expand the dataset
    D) To perform clustering analysis

14. What is the role of singular value decomposition (SVD) in data analysis?
    A) It helps in clustering data points
    B) It assists in reducing noise in data
    C) It decomposes a matrix into singular vectors and singular values
    D) It performs polynomial regression

15. Which of the following is not a step in the data science workflow?
    A) Data acquisition
    B) smallsing
    C) Data visualization
    D) Data fabrication

16. What is the purpose of regularization in machine learning?
    A) To make the model overfit the training data
    B) To penalize large coefficients in the model
    C) To increase the bias of the model
    D) To decrease the variance of the model

17. Which statistical concept measures the spread of data points around the mean?
    A) Median
    B) Variance
    C) Mean absolute deviation
    D) Mode

18. What is the formula for the dot product of two vectors A and B?
    A) $|A| \times |B| \cos(\theta)$
    B) $|A| + |B|$
    C) $|A| \times |B|$
    D) $|A| - |B| \cos(\theta)$

19. Which algorithm is used to find the optimal solution for linear regression?
    A) Gradient Descent
    B) Breadth-First Search
    C) Depth-First Search
    D) K-nearest Neighbors

20. What is the purpose of the bias term in linear regression?
    A) To offset the influence of independent variables
    B) To add noise to the model
    C) To improve model generalization
    D) To create a curved relationship between variables

Chapter 2

Foundations of Statistical Analysis

2.1 Statistical Modelling

Statistical modeling is essential in data science for making predictions and drawing inferences from data. It involves three key steps: model formulation, parameter estimation, and model evaluation.

Formulating a statistical model starts with identifying relevant variables and specifying their relationships, using techniques such as linear regression, logistic regression, decision trees, and neural networks. The goal is to capture the data's underlying structure to make accurate predictions or inferences.

Once the model is formulated, the next step is parameter estimation. This involves fitting the model to the data to find the best parameter values, using methods like maximum likelihood estimation, Bayesian inference, and Markov Chain Monte Carlo.

Finally, the model's predictive power and generalizability are evaluated. This step assesses how well the model predicts new data or draws inferences about the population, using techniques such as cross-validation, hypothesis testing, and information criteria.

Statistical modeling is widely used in data science for applications like predictive modeling, regression analysis, classification, and clustering. Techniques like linear regression, logistic regression, decision trees, random forests, and neural networks are common, helping to identify patterns in complex datasets and make reliable predictions.

2.2 Random Variables

In probability theory and statistics, a random variable is a variable that can take on different values in a given range with a certain probability distribution.

Random variables are used to model uncertain or random phenomena, and they are essential in many applications of data science, such as hypothesis testing, regression analysis, and machine learning. There are two main types of random variables: discrete random variables and continuous random variables. A discrete random variable can only take on a finite or countably infinite set of values. Examples of discrete random variables include the number of heads in a coin toss, the number of cars passing through a toll booth in a given time interval, or the number of patients with a certain disease in a population. A continuous random variable can take on any value within a continuous range. Examples of continuous random variables include the height of a person, the time it takes for a bus to arrive at a stop, or the temperature of a room. Random variables are characterized by their probability distribution, which describes the likelihood of the variable taking on a certain value or set of values. The probability distribution can be described by various parameters, such as the mean, variance, and standard deviation. The concept of random variables is fundamental in statistical inference, which involves making inferences about a population based on a sample of data. In this context, random variables are used to model the underlying distribution of the population, and statistical methods are used to make inferences about the population based on the sample data.

2.3 Probability Mass/Density Functions

In probability theory, a probability mass function (PMF) is a function that gives the probability that a discrete random variable is equal to a particular value. A probability density function (PDF) is a function that gives the probability that a continuous random variable takes on a particular value.

The PMF and PDF describe the probability distribution of a random variable, which specifies the probabilities associated with the possible outcomes of the random variable. The PMF and PDF are normalized, meaning that the probabilities they assign sum or integrate to 1 over the entire range of the random variable.

Table 2.1: Differences between PMF and PDF

	PMF (Probability Mass Function)	**PDF (Probability Density Function)**
Definition	Discrete random variables	Continuous random variables
Domain	Finite or countably infinite	Continuous
Value	Actual probability at each point	Represents relative likelihood
Example	Coin toss, Dice roll	Normal distribution, Exponential distribution

For a discrete random variable, the PMF gives the probability of each possible outcome. For example, if X is a random variable that takes on the values 1, 2, and 3 with probabilities 0.2, 0.3, and 0.5, respectively, then the PMF of X is given by:

$$P(X = 1) = 0.2$$
$$P(X = 2) = 0.3$$
$$P(X = 3) = 0.5$$

For a continuous random variable, the PDF gives the probability density at each point in the range of the random variable. The probability of a particular value is given by the area under the curve of the PDF over that value. For example, if X is a continuous random variable with PDF $f(x) = 2x$, for $0 < x < 1$, then the probability of X being between 0.2 and 0.6 is given by:

$$P(0.2 < X < 0.6) = \int_{0.2}^{0.6} 2x\,dx = 0.28$$

2.4 Sample Statistics

In statistics, a sample statistic is a value that is calculated from a sample of data, and is used to estimate an unknown population parameter. Sample statistics are used in inferential statistics, which involves making inferences about a population based on a sample of data.

Common sample statistics include:

- **Sample mean:** The sample mean is the average of a set of sample values. It is a common measure of central tendency, and is used to estimate the population mean.
- **Sample variance:** The sample variance is a measure of the variability of the sample values. It is used to estimate the population variance.
- **Sample standard deviation:** The sample standard deviation is the square root of the sample variance. It is also a measure of the variability of the sample values, and is used to estimate the population standard deviation.
- **Sample proportion:** The sample proportion is the proportion of sample values that have a certain characteristic. It is used to estimate the population proportion.
- **Sample correlation coefficient:** The sample correlation coefficient is a measure of the linear relationship between two variables in a sample. It is used to estimate the population correlation coefficient.

Sample statistics can be used to make inferences about population parameters using statistical tests and confidence intervals. These techniques allow analysts to estimate the range of likely values for a population parameter based on the sample statistic, and to test hypotheses about the population based on the sample data.

2.5 Hypothesis Testing

Hypothesis testing is a statistical method used in data science to make decisions about whether a particular hypothesis about a population is supported by the available evidence. A hypothesis is a statement about the population that is being studied, and a hypothesis test is a procedure to determine whether the evidence supports or contradicts the hypothesis.

The hypothesis testing process involves the following steps:

1. **State the null hypothesis:** This is the hypothesis that is assumed to be true, typically denoted by H_0. It represents the status quo or default assumption and is the hypothesis that will be tested against an alternative hypothesis.

2. **State the alternative hypothesis:** This is the hypothesis that is being tested, typically denoted by H_a. It represents the hypothesis that is being proposed as an alternative to the null hypothesis.

3. **Choose a significance level:** This is the probability threshold used to determine whether to reject the null hypothesis, typically denoted by alpha (α). It is set in advance by the analyst.

4. **Collect and analyze data:** Data is collected and analyzed to obtain a sample statistic, which is used to estimate the population parameter of interest.

5. **Calculate the test statistic:** The test statistic is a measure of the distance between the sample statistic and the null hypothesis value and is used to determine the likelihood of observing the sample statistic under the null hypothesis.

6. **Determine the p-value:** The p-value is the probability of observing a test statistic as extreme or more extreme than the observed value, assuming the null hypothesis is true.

7. **Make a decision:** The decision is made by comparing the p-value to the significance level. If the p-value is less than or equal to the significance level, the null hypothesis is rejected in favor of the alternative hypothesis. If the p-value is greater than the significance level, the null hypothesis is not rejected.

2.6 Exercises

2.6.1 Short and Long Answer Questions

1. Define a random variable and provide an example of its application in a real-world scenario.

2. Explain the difference between a probability mass function (PMF) and a probability density function (PDF), and give examples of each.

3. Calculate the mean, median, and mode for the dataset: $\{4, 5, 6, 6, 7, 8, 9\}$.

4. Describe the process of hypothesis testing and provide an example where it might be used.

5. Differentiate between Type I and Type II errors in hypothesis testing, and explain their practical implications.

6. Determine the critical value for a hypothesis test with a significance level of 0.05 and 10 degrees of freedom.

7. Compute the p-value for a hypothesis test given a test statistic of 2.45 and a significance level of 0.01.

8. Compare and contrast sample statistics and population parameters, providing examples of each.

9. Define the concept of a confidence interval and explain how it is used in statistical inference.

10. Perform a chi-square test for independence using the following contingency table:

	Group A	Group B
Outcome 1	25	35
Outcome 2	30	40

2.6.2 Fill in the Blanks

1. Random variables can be characterized by their probability ______.

2. Probability mass functions (PMFs) describe the probabilities associated with ______ random variables.

3. Sample statistics are numerical values calculated from a ______.

4. Hypothesis testing is a statistical method used to evaluate the validity of ______.

5. Type I error occurs when the null hypothesis is ______.

6. The chi-square test is used to analyze the ______ between categorical variables.

7. The critical value in hypothesis testing helps determine the ______.

8. Parametric statistical tests assume that the distribution of data is ______.

9. Confidence intervals are used to estimate ______ from sample statistics.

10. The standard error of the mean is the standard deviation of the distribution of ______.

2.6.3 Multiple Choice Questions

1. What is a random variable?
   A) A variable with a fixed value
   B) A variable whose outcome is determined by chance
   C) A variable with infinite possibilities
   D) A variable that cannot be measured

2. Which of the following represents a discrete random variable?
   A) Height of a person
   B) Weight of a fruit
   C) Number of heads in coin toss
   D) Temperature in Celsius

3. What is a probability mass function (PMF)?
   A) A function that describes the likelihood of continuous variables
   B) A function that describes the probability distribution of discrete random variables
   C) A function that calculates the mean of a sample
   D) A function that measures the spread of data

4. What does the probability density function (PDF) represent?
   A) The cumulative probability of a continuous random variable
   B) The probability mass of a discrete random variable
   C) The likelihood of observing a specific value of a continuous random variable
   D) The spread of data in a sample

5. Which of the following is a measure of central tendency?
   A) Variance
   B) Standard deviation
   C) Mean
   D) Median

6. What is the median?
   A) The most frequent value in a dataset
   B) The arithmetic average of a dataset
   C) The middle value of a sorted dataset
   D) The difference between the largest and smallest values in a dataset

7. What is the purpose of hypothesis testing?
   A) To prove a hypothesis
   B) To disprove a hypothesis
   C) To calculate the mean of a population
   D) To estimate the standard deviation of a sample

8. What is a null hypothesis?
   A) A hypothesis that is proven to be true
   B) A hypothesis that is assumed to be true
   C) A hypothesis that is always false
   D) A hypothesis that has no relevance

9. What is a p-value in hypothesis testing?
   A) The probability of rejecting the null hypothesis when it is true
   B) The probability of accepting the null hypothesis when it is false
   C) The probability of accepting the alternative hypothesis when it is true
   D) The probability of failing to reject the null hypothesis when it is true

10. What does Type I error represent in hypothesis testing?
    A) Rejecting the null hypothesis when it is true
    B) Accepting the null hypothesis when it is false
    C) Rejecting the alternative hypothesis when it is true
    D) Accepting the alternative hypothesis when it is false

11. What is Type II error in hypothesis testing?
    A) Accepting the null hypothesis when it is true
    B) Rejecting the null hypothesis when it is false
    C) Accepting the alternative hypothesis when it is true
    D) Rejecting the alternative hypothesis when it is false

12. Which statistical test is appropriate for comparing means of two independent groups?
    A) Paired t-test
    B) One-sample t-test
    C) Independent samples t-test
    D) Chi-square test

13. What is the purpose of the chi-square test?
    A) To compare means of two independent groups
    B) To compare means of two dependent groups
    C) To test for association between categorical variables
    D) To test for normality of a distribution

14. In the chi-square test, what does the chi-square statistic measure?
    A) The difference between observed and expected frequencies
    B) The difference between means of two independent groups
    C) The difference between means of two dependent groups
    D) The difference between the sample mean and population mean

15. What is the critical value in hypothesis testing?
    A) The value of the test statistic that determines the rejection region
    B) The value of the null hypothesis
    C) The value of the alternative hypothesis
    D) The value of the sample mean

16. Which of the following is a parametric statistical test?
    A) Wilcoxon signed-rank test
    B) Mann-Whitney U test
    C) Analysis of Variance (ANOVA)
    D) Kruskal-Wallis test

17. What is the assumption of normality in parametric tests?
    A) The distribution of data is normal
    B) The distribution of data is not normal
    C) The distribution of data is positively skewed
    D) The distribution of data is negatively skewed

18. Which statistical method is used to estimate the population parameters from sample statistics?
    A) Hypothesis testing
    B) Confidence intervals
    C) Chi-square test
    D) Analysis of Variance (ANOVA)

19. What is the standard error of the mean?
    A) The standard deviation of the population
    B) The standard deviation of the sample
    C) The standard deviation of the distribution of sample means
    D) The standard deviation of the distribution of sample variances

Chapter 3

Predictive Modelling

3.1 Predictive Modelling

Predictive modeling is a process used in data science to build mathematical models that can predict future outcomes based on historical data. It involves using statistical techniques to analyze data and create models that can be used to make predictions about future events or behavior.

The process of predictive modeling typically involves the following steps:

1. **Define the problem:** This involves defining the problem that needs to be solved and identifying the data that will be used to build the model.

2. **Collect and preprocess the data:** Data is collected from various sources and preprocessed to ensure it is clean and usable.

3. **Explore and analyze the data:** The data is analyzed to identify patterns, correlations, and other insights that can be used to build the model.

4. **Choose a modeling technique:** Based on the nature of the problem and the data available, a suitable modeling technique is chosen. This can include linear regression, decision trees, neural networks, or other methods.

5. **Train and validate the model:** The model is trained using historical data and validated to ensure it is accurate and reliable.

6. **Deploy and monitor the model:** The model is deployed in a production environment and monitored to ensure it continues to perform well over time.

Predictive modeling is used in a wide range of applications, including finance, marketing, healthcare, and many others. It can be used to predict customer behavior, identify potential fraud, optimize marketing campaigns, and more. The accuracy of the model depends on the quality of the data, the modeling technique used, and the validation process, among other factors. Effective predictive modeling can help organizations make better decisions, optimize their operations, and gain a competitive edge in the marketplace.

3.2 Linear Regression

Linear regression is a statistical technique used in data science to model the relationship between a dependent variable and one or more independent variables. It is a simple yet powerful method for predicting a continuous numerical outcome based on one or more predictors.

In linear regression, the goal is to find a straight line that best fits the data, such that the distance between the predicted values and the actual values is minimized. This line is called the regression line, and it represents the relationship between the dependent variable and the independent variables.

The regression line is typically represented using the equation:

$$y = mx + b$$

where y is the dependent variable, x is the independent variable, m is the slope of the line, and b is the y-intercept.

3.3 Simple Linear Regression Model Building

Building a simple linear regression model involves the following steps:

1. **Collect and preprocess the data:** Data is collected from various sources and preprocessed to ensure it is clean and usable. In simple linear regression, there are two variables: the dependent variable (y) and the independent variable (x).

2. **Explore and analyze the data:** The data is analyzed to identify patterns, correlations, and other insights that can be used to build the model. This can involve visualizing the data using scatter plots and other techniques.

3. **Choose the independent variable:** Based on the problem and the data available, a suitable independent variable is chosen. In simple linear regression, there is only one independent variable.

4. **Fit the regression line:** The regression line is fit to the data using techniques such as ordinary least squares regression. This involves finding the values of the slope (m) and y-intercept (b) that best fit the data.

5. **Evaluate the model:** The model is evaluated using metrics such as the coefficient of determination (R-squared) and root mean squared error (RMSE) to assess how well it fits the data.

6. **Use the model to make predictions:** The model can be used to make predictions on new data by plugging in the values of the independent variable.

3.3.1 The Regression Equation in Matrix Form

With multiple regression, there is one dependent variable and k independent variables. The regression equation is:

$$\hat{y} = b_0 + b_1 x_1 + b_2 x_2 + \ldots + b_{k-1} x_{k-1} + b_k x_k$$

where $\hat{y}$ is the predicted value of the dependent variable, b_k are regression coefficients, and x_k is the value of independent variable k.

To express the regression equation in matrix form, we need to define three matrices: Y, b, and X.

$$Y = \begin{bmatrix} y_1 \\ y_2 \\ \vdots \\ y_n \end{bmatrix}$$

$$b = \begin{bmatrix} b_0 \\ b_1 \\ \vdots \\ b_k \end{bmatrix}$$

$$X = \begin{bmatrix} 1 & x_{1,1} & x_{1,2} & \cdots & x_{1,k} \\ 1 & x_{2,1} & x_{2,2} & \cdots & x_{2,k} \\ \vdots & \vdots & \vdots & \ddots & \vdots \\ 1 & x_{n,1} & x_{n,2} & \cdots & x_{n,k} \end{bmatrix}$$

Here, the dataset consists of n records. Each record includes scores for one dependent variable and k independent variables. Y is an $n \times 1$ vector that holds predicted values of the dependent variable; and b is a $(k+1) \times 1$ vector that holds estimated regression coefficients. Matrix X has a column of 1's plus k columns of values for each independent variable in the regression equation.

Given these matrices, the multiple regression equation can be expressed concisely as:

$$Y = Xb$$

Normal Equations in Matrix Form:

Just as the regression equation can be expressed compactly in matrix form, so can the normal equations. The least squares normal equations can be expressed as:

$$X^T Y = X^T X b \quad \text{or} \quad X^T X b = X^T Y$$

Here, matrix X^T is the transpose of matrix X. To solve for regression coefficients, simply pre-multiply by the inverse of $X^T X$:

$$(X^T X)^{-1} X^T X b = (X^T X)^{-1} X^T Y$$

$$b = (X^T X)^{-1} X^T Y$$

where $(X^T X)^{-1} X^T X = I$, the identity matrix.

In the real world, you will probably never compute regression coefficients by hand. Generally, you will use software like SAS, SPSS, Minitab, or Excel. In the problem below, however, we will compute regression coefficients manually so you will understand what is going on.

In R, you can build a simple linear regression model using the `lm()` function, which stands for linear model. Here is an example of building a simple linear regression model using R:

```
# create some example data
x <- c(1, 2, 3, 4, 5)
y <- c(2, 4, 5, 4, 6)

# fit a linear regression model to the data
model <- lm(y ~ x)

# print the summary of the model
summary(model)

# use the model to make predictions on new data
x_new <- c(6, 7, 8)
y_pred <- predict(model, data.frame(x = x_new))
print(y_pred)
```

This code creates some example data, fits a linear regression model to it using the `lm()` function, prints the summary of the model using the `summary()` function, and uses the model to make predictions on new data using the `predict()` function.

The output of the `summary()` function includes various statistics such as the coefficient estimates, standard error, t-value, and p-value for the intercept and slope of the regression line, as well as the R-squared value and adjusted R-squared value. These statistics can be used to evaluate the fit of the model and the significance of the relationship between the independent and dependent variables.

The `predict()` function is used to make predictions on new data. In this example, we create a vector of new values for the independent variable (`x_new`) and use the `predict()` function to get the corresponding predicted values of the dependent variable (`y_pred`).

3.4 Multiple Linear Regression

Multiple linear regression is a statistical technique used to model the relationship between two or more independent variables and a dependent variable. It is an extension of simple linear regression, where there is only one independent variable.

The general equation for multiple linear regression is:

$$y = b_0 + b_1x_1 + b_2x_2 + ... + b_nx_n + \epsilon$$

where y is the dependent variable, $x_1, x_2, ..., x_n$ are the independent variables, $b_0, b_1, b_2, ..., b_n$ are the coefficients of the independent variables, and ϵ is the error term.

```
# load the dataset
data <- read.csv("data.csv")

# fit the regression model
model <- lm(y ~ x1 + x2 + x3, data = data)

# print the coefficients of the regression line
coef(model)

# predict on new data
new_data <- data.frame(x1 = c(1, 2, 3),
                       x2 = c(4, 5, 6),
                       x3 = c(7, 8, 9))
predict(model, new_data)
```

This code loads a dataset from a CSV file, fits a multiple linear regression model to the data using the `lm` function, prints the coefficients of the regression line using the `coef` function, and uses the model to make predictions on new data using the `predict` function.

The formula used in the `lm` function specifies the dependent variable (y) and the independent variables (x_1, x_2, and x_3) as follows:

$$y \sim x_1 + x_2 + x_3$$

This formula can be modified to include or exclude other variables or to include interactions between variables.

Note that it is important to preprocess the data before fitting a multiple linear regression model, including handling missing values and scaling the variables if necessary. Also, it is important to check the assumptions of the model, such as linearity, normality, and homoscedasticity, using diagnostic plots and statistical tests.

3.5 Logistic Regression

Logistic regression is a popular statistical method for analyzing binary or categorical outcome variables. It models the relationship between a binary response variable and one or more predictor variables, usually using a sigmoid or logistic function to model the probability of the response variable taking on a certain value.

Here's an example of how to build a logistic regression model in R:

```
# load the dataset
data <- read.csv("data.csv")

# fit the logistic regression model
model <- glm(y ~ x1 + x2 + x3, data = data, family = binomial())

# print the coefficients of the model
coef(model)

# predict on new data
new_data <- data.frame(x1 = c(1, 2, 3),
                       x2 = c(4, 5, 6),
                        x3 = c(7, 8, 9))
predict(model, new_data, type = "response")
```

This code loads a dataset from a CSV file, fits a logistic regression model to the data using the `glm` function, prints the coefficients of the model using the `coef` function, and uses the model to make predictions on new data using the `predict` function.

The formula used in the `glm` function specifies the dependent variable (y) and the independent variables (x_1, x_2, and x_3) as follows:

$$y \sim x_1 + x_2 + x_3$$

This formula can be modified to include or exclude other variables, or to include interactions between variables.

The `family` argument in the `glm` function specifies the type of model to be fit. For logistic regression, we use `binomial()`, which indicates that we want to fit a logistic regression model.

Note that it is important to preprocess the data before fitting a logistic regression model, including handling missing values and scaling the variables if necessary. Also, it is important to check the assumptions of the model, such as linearity, independence, and absence of multicollinearity, using diagnostic plots and statistical tests.

Metrics for regression models serve to quantify the performance and accuracy of predictions for continuous numerical outcomes. Mean Absolute Error (MAE) calculates the average of absolute differences between predicted and actual values, offering insight into the typical magnitude of errors. Mean Squared Error (MSE) computes the average of squared differences, emphasizing larger errors more than MAE. Root Mean Squared Error (RMSE), the square root of MSE, provides an interpretable measure in the same unit as the target variable. R-squared (R^2) gauges the proportion of variance in the dependent variable explained by the independent variables, with values ranging from 0 to 1 indicating perfect to no linear relationship. These metrics collectively aid in assessing regression model fit and predictive accuracy, guiding model selection and refinement based on specific problem requirements.

Table 3.1: Formulas for Regression Metrics

Metric	**Formula**
Mean Absolute Error (MAE)	$\text{MAE} = \frac{1}{n}\sum_{i=1}^{n} \lvert y_i - \hat{y}_i \rvert$
Mean Squared Error (MSE)	$\text{MSE} = \frac{1}{n}\sum_{i=1}^{n} (y_i - \hat{y}_i)^2$
Root Mean Squared Error (RMSE)	$\text{RMSE} = \sqrt{\text{MSE}}$
R-squared (R2)	$R^2 = 1 - \frac{\sum_{i=1}^{n}(y_i - \hat{y}_i)^2}{\sum_{i=1}^{n}(y_i - \bar{y})^2}$

3.6 Building SLR Example

Given data:

$$X = \{1, 2, 4, 3, 5\}$$

$$Y = \{1, 3, 3, 2, 5\}$$

Step 1: Compute necessary sums:

$$\begin{aligned} n &= 5 \\ \sum X &= 1 + 2 + 4 + 3 + 5 = 15 \\ \sum Y &= 1 + 3 + 3 + 2 + 5 = 14 \\ \sum XY &= (1 \times 1) + (2 \times 3) + (4 \times 3) + (3 \times 2) + (5 \times 5) = 50 \\ \sum X^2 &= 1^2 + 2^2 + 4^2 + 3^2 + 5^2 = 55 \end{aligned}$$

Step 2: Compute slope b_1 and y-intercept b_0:

$$b_1 = \frac{(5 \times 50) - (15 \times 14)}{(5 \times 55) - (15)^2}$$
$$b_0 = \frac{14 - b_1 \times 15}{5}$$

Now, we compute b_1:

$$b_1 = \frac{250 - 210}{275 - 225} = \frac{40}{50} = 0.8$$

Next, we compute b_0:

$$b_0 = \frac{14 - (0.8 \times 15)}{5} = \frac{14 - 12}{5} = 0.4$$

So, the linear regression model is:

$$\hat{Y} = 0.8X + 0.4$$

Step 3: Compute predicted values $\hat{Y}$ using the linear regression model:

$$\hat{Y}_1 = (0.8 \times 1) + 0.4 = 1.2$$
$$\hat{Y}_2 = (0.8 \times 2) + 0.4 = 2.0$$
$$\hat{Y}_3 = (0.8 \times 4) + 0.4 = 3.6$$
$$\hat{Y}_4 = (0.8 \times 3) + 0.4 = 2.8$$
$$\hat{Y}_5 = (0.8 \times 5) + 0.4 = 4.0$$

Step 4: Compute RMSE (Root Mean Squared Error):

$$\begin{aligned}
\text{RMSE} &= \sqrt{\frac{1}{n}\sum_{i=1}^{n}(Y_i - \hat{Y}_i)^2} \\
&= \sqrt{\frac{(1-1.2)^2 + (3-2.0)^2 + (3-3.6)^2 + (2-2.8)^2 + (5-4.0)^2}{5}} \\
&= \sqrt{\frac{0.04 + 1 + 0.36 + 0.64 + 1}{5}} \\
&= \sqrt{\frac{3.04}{5}} \\
&\approx \sqrt{0.608} \approx 0.78
\end{aligned}$$

Step 5: Compute R^2 (R-squared):

$$\begin{aligned}
R^2 &= 1 - \frac{\sum_{i=1}^{n}(Y_i - \hat{Y}_i)^2}{\sum_{i=1}^{n}(Y_i - \bar{Y})^2} \\
&= 1 - \frac{(1-1.2)^2 + (3-2.0)^2 + (3-3.6)^2 + (2-2.8)^2 + (5-4.0)^2}{(1-2)^2 + (3-2)^2 + (3-2)^2 + (2-2)^2 + (5-2)^2} \\
&= 1 - \frac{0.04 + 1 + 0.36 + 0.64 + 1}{1+1+1+0+9} \\
&= 1 - \frac{3.04}{12} \\
&= 1 - 0.2533 \\
&\approx 0.7467
\end{aligned}$$

3.7 Building MLR Example

Consider the table below. It shows three performance measures for five students:

Student	Test score	IQ	Study hours
1	100	110	40
2	90	120	30
3	80	100	20
4	70	90	0
5	60	80	10

Using least squares regression, we want to develop a regression equation to predict test scores based on (1) IQ and (2) the number of hours that the student studied.

For this problem, we have some raw data, and we want to use this raw data to define a least-squares regression equation:

$$\hat{y} = b_0 + b_1 x_1 + b_2 x_2$$

where $\hat{y}$ is the predicted test score; b_0, b_1, and b_2 are regression coefficients; x_1 is an IQ score; and x_2 is the number of hours that the student studied.

On the right side of the equation, the only unknowns are the regression coefficients. To define the regression coefficients, we use the following equation:

$$b = (X'X)^{-1}X'Y$$

To solve this equation, we need to complete the following steps:

1. Define X.
2. Define X'.
3. Compute $X'X$.

4. Find the inverse of $X'X$.
5. Define Y.

Let's begin with matrix X. Matrix X has a column of 1's plus two columns of values for each independent variable. So, this is matrix X and its transpose X':

$$X = \begin{bmatrix} 1 & 110 & 40 \\ 1 & 120 & 30 \\ 1 & 100 & 20 \\ 1 & 90 & 0 \\ 1 & 80 & 10 \end{bmatrix}$$

$$X' = \begin{bmatrix} 1 & 1 & 1 & 1 & 1 \\ 110 & 120 & 100 & 90 & 80 \\ 40 & 30 & 20 & 0 & 10 \end{bmatrix}$$

Given X' and X, it is a simple matter to compute $X'X$:

$$X'X = \begin{bmatrix} 5 & 500 & 100 \\ 500 & 51,000 & 10,800 \\ 100 & 10,800 & 3,000 \end{bmatrix}$$

Finding the inverse of $X'X$ takes a little more effort. A way to find the inverse is described on this site at `https://stattrek.com/matrix-algebra/how-to-find-inverse`. Ultimately, we find:

$$(X'X)^{-1} = \begin{bmatrix} \frac{101}{5} & -\frac{7}{30} & \frac{1}{6} \\ -\frac{7}{30} & \frac{1}{360} & -\frac{1}{450} \\ \frac{1}{6} & -\frac{1}{450} & \frac{1}{360} \end{bmatrix}$$

Next, we define Y, the vector of dependent variable scores. For this problem, it is the vector of test scores:

$$Y = \begin{bmatrix} 100 \\ 90 \\ 80 \\ 70 \\ 60 \end{bmatrix}$$

With all of the essential matrices defined, we are ready to compute the least squares regression coefficients:

$$b = (X'X)^{-1}X'Y$$

$$b = \begin{bmatrix} b_0 \\ b_1 \\ b_2 \end{bmatrix} = \begin{bmatrix} 20 \\ 0.5 \\ 0.5 \end{bmatrix}$$

To conclude, here is our least-squares regression equation:

$$\hat{y} = 20 + 0.5x_1 + 0.5x_2$$

where $\hat{y}$ is the predicted test score; x_1 is an IQ score; and x_2 is the number of hours that the student studied. The regression coefficients are $b_0 = 20$, $b_1 = 0.5$, and $b_2 = 0.5$.

3.8 Multinomial regression

Multinomial regression is a type of regression analysis used to model the relationship between multiple independent variables and a categorical dependent variable with more than two categories. It is an extension of binary logistic regression to handle multiple categories.

Model Formulation: In multinomial regression, we have:

1. Dependent Variable (Response Variable): A categorical variable with more than two categories.

2. Independent Variables (Predictors): One or more independent variables that are used to predict the probabilities of each category of the dependent variable.

Model Assumptions: Multinomial logistic regression makes several assumptions, including:

1. Independence of observations: Each observation is independent of the others.

2. Linearity: The relationship between the independent variables and the logits (log-odds) of the dependent variable is linear.

3. No multicollinearity: The independent variables are not highly correlated with each other.

4. No perfect separation: There are no categories of the dependent variable that can be perfectly predicted by the independent variables.

Implementation in R:

In R, multinomial regression can be implemented using the multinom() function from the nnet package or using the glm() function with the family = "multinomial" argument.

```
# Install and load the nnet package
install.packages("nnet")
library(nnet)

# Fit multinomial logistic regression model
```

```
model <- multinom(factor_response_variable ~ ., data = your_data)

# Summary of the model
summary(model)
```

glm() from the base package:

```
# Fit multinomial logistic regression model
model <- glm(factor_response_variable ~ ., data = your_data,
family = "multinomial")
# Summary of the model
summary(model)
```

Replace `factor_response_variable` with the factor variable you want to predict, and `your_data` with your dataset. Ensure that your response variable is a factor with multiple levels, indicating the different classes or categories you are predicting.

3.9 Exercises

3.9.1 Short and Long Answer Questions

1. Define linear regression and explain its primary use in predictive modelling. Provide a real-world example.

2. What is the difference between simple linear regression and multiple linear regression? Provide equations for both types of regression.

3. Discuss the assumptions of linear regression and how they can impact the accuracy of the model.

4. Calculate the coefficient of determination (R-squared) for a linear regression model with the following data points: $\{(1, 2), (2, 3), (3, 4), (4, 5)\}$.

5. Explain the concept of logistic regression and its application in predictive modelling. Provide an example dataset where logistic regression would be suitable.

6. Describe the process of model building in predictive modelling. What are the key steps involved?

7. Compare and contrast the strengths and weaknesses of linear regression and logistic regression models.

8. For a simple linear regression model with coefficients $\beta_0 = 3$ and $\beta_1 = 2$, predict the value of the dependent variable (Y) when the independent variable (X) is 5.

9. How does multicollinearity impact the results of a multiple linear regression model? Provide strategies to address multicollinearity.

10. Evaluate the performance of a logistic regression model using the confusion matrix generated from the following data:

Actual Class	Predicted Class
Positive	Positive
Negative	Positive
Positive	Negative
Negative	Negative
Positive	Positive
Negative	Negative

3.9.2 Fill in the Blanks

1. Linear regression is used for ______.

2. The basic assumption of simple linear regression is that the relationship between variables is ______.

3. The equation of a simple linear regression model is $y =$ ______.

4. The purpose of multiple linear regression is to model relationships between ______.

5. The difference between linear regression and logistic regression is that linear regression predicts ______, while logistic regression predicts ______.

6. The range of values that logistic regression predicts is ______.

7. The Sigmoid function used in logistic regression is used to transform the linear combination of predictors into a ______.

8. The coefficient of determination (R^2) in linear regression represents the proportion of variance in the dependent variable explained by the ______.

9. Multicollinearity in multiple linear regression occurs when there is ______ between the independent variables.

10. Residual analysis in regression modeling is used to check for ______.

3.9.3 Multiple Choice Questions

1. What is linear regression used for?
   A) Classifying data
   B) Predicting continuous outcomes
   C) Analyzing categorical variables
   D) Finding outliers in data

2. What is the basic assumption of simple linear regression?
   A) The relationship between variables is linear
   B) There is no relationship between variables
   C) The relationship between variables is exponential
   D) The relationship between variables is quadratic

3. What is the equation of a simple linear regression model?
   A) $y = mx + b$
   B) $y = ax^2 + bx + c$
   C) $y = e^x$
   D) $y = \frac{1}{1+e^{-z}}$

4. What is the purpose of multiple linear regression?
   A) To model relationships between multiple independent variables and one dependent variable
   B) To model relationships between one independent variable and multiple dependent variables
   C) To model relationships between multiple independent variables and multiple dependent variables
   D) To model relationships between categorical variables

5. What is the difference between linear regression and logistic regression?
   A) Linear regression predicts continuous outcomes, while logistic regression predicts categorical outcomes
   B) Linear regression predicts categorical outcomes, while logistic regression predicts continuous outcomes
   C) Linear regression cannot handle multiple independent variables, while logistic regression can
   D) Logistic regression is only used for binary classification problems

6. What is the range of values that logistic regression predicts?
   A) $(-\infty, +\infty)$
   B) $[0, 1]$
   C) $(-1, 1)$
   D) $(0, +\infty)$

7. What is the Sigmoid function used for in logistic regression?
   A) To calculate the residuals
   B) To calculate the coefficients
   C) To transform the linear combination of predictors into a probability
   D) To handle missing values

8. What does the coefficient of determination (R^2) represent in linear regression?
   A) The proportion of variance in the dependent variable explained by the independent variable
   B) The proportion of variance in the independent variable explained by the dependent variable
   C) The correlation between the independent and dependent variables
   D) The sum of squared errors

9. What is multicollinearity in multiple linear regression?
   A) A situation where there is perfect correlation between the independent variables
   B) A situation where there is no correlation between the independent variables
   C) A situation where the dependent variable is correlated with the independent variables
   D) A situation where the residuals are normally distributed

10. What is the purpose of residual analysis in regression modeling?
   A) To check for multicollinearity
   B) To check for normality of residuals
   C) To check for linearity of the relationship
   D) To check for heteroscedasticity

11. What is heteroscedasticity in regression analysis?
   A) A situation where the residuals have a constant variance across all values of the independent variable
   B) A situation where the residuals have a non-constant variance across different values of the independent variable
   C) A situation where the residuals are normally distributed
   D) A situation where the residuals are not normally distributed

12. Which of the following techniques can be used to handle multicollinearity?
   A) Principal Component Analysis (PCA)
   B) Stepwise regression
   C) Ridge regression
   D) Lasso regression

13. What is the purpose of feature scaling in regression modeling?
   A) To reduce the dimensionality of the dataset
   B) To standardize the range of values of independent variables
   C) To increase the complexity of the model
   D) To improve the interpretability of the model

14. What does the p-value represent in regression analysis?
    A) The strength of the relationship between variables
    B) The significance of the coefficient
    C) The proportion of variance explained by the model
    D) The range of values of the dependent variable

15. In logistic regression, what is the logit function?
    A) $log(p)$
    B) $log(1-p)$
    C) p^2
    D) e^p

16. Which of the following is not an assumption of linear regression?
    A) Linearity
    B) Normality of residuals
    C) Homoscedasticity
    D) Independence of observations

17. How is the goodness of fit of logistic regression models evaluated?
    A) R-squared
    B) Mean Squared Error
    C) Area Under the ROC Curve (AUC)
    D) Root Mean Squared Error

18. What is the purpose of regularization techniques like Ridge and Lasso regression?
    A) To increase the bias of the model
    B) To reduce overfitting
    C) To increase the complexity of the model
    D) To introduce more predictors

19. Which type of regression is suitable for modeling binary outcomes?
    A) Simple linear regression
    B) Multiple linear regression
    C) Logistic regression
    D) Ridge regression

Chapter 4

Introduction to R Programming

4.1 Introduction to R Programming

R serves as an open-source programming language and software environment tailored for statistical computing, data analysis, and visualization. It offers an extensive array of statistical and graphical techniques, encompassing linear and nonlinear modeling, time-series analysis, clustering, and machine-learning algorithms. With widespread adoption across academia, research, and industry, R benefits from a substantial and engaged user community, which actively participates in its ongoing development and upkeep.

Here are some basic concepts in R programming:

- **R data types:** R has several data types, including numeric, character, logical, and factors. Numeric data types represent real or complex numbers, while character data types represent strings of characters.Logical data types represent true or false values, and factors represent categorical data.
- **R variables:** In R, variables are used to store data values of different types. You can create variables using the assignment operator ¡- or =. For example, `x <- 5` creates a variable named `x` and assigns the value 5 to it.
- **R functions:** Functions are blocks of code that perform a specific task. R has many built-in functions, and you can also create your own functions using the `function` keyword. For example, `mean(x)` calculates the mean of the numeric vector `x`.
- **R packages:** R packages consist of sets of functions, data & documentation aimed at expanding R's capabilities. To integrate these packages, utilize

the `install.packages()` function for installation and the `library()` function to incorporate them into your R session.

- **R control structures:** Control structures are used to control the flow of execution in R. The most common control structures are if-else, for, while, and repeat loops.

```
# create a numeric vector
x <- c(1, 2, 3, 4, 5)

# calculate the mean of the vector
mean(x)

# create a function that calculates the sum of two numbers
sum_numbers <- function(a, b) {
  sum <- a + b
  return(sum)
}

# use the function to calculate the sum of two numbers
sum_numbers(3, 5)

# install and load the ggplot2 package
install.packages("ggplot2")
library(ggplot2)

# create a scatter plot of x and y data
x <- c(1, 2, 3, 4, 5)
y <- c(10, 8, 6, 4, 2)
ggplot(data.frame(x, y), aes(x, y)) + geom_point()

# create a for loop that prints the numbers from 1 to 5
for (i in 1:5) {
  print(i)
}
```

This code creates a numeric vector `x`, calculates its mean using the `mean()` function, creates a custom function `sum_numbers()` that calculates the sum of two numbers, installs and loads the `ggplot2` package to create a scatter plot, and creates a `for` loop that prints the numbers from 1 to 5.

4.2 Installation of R S/W using the interface

To get started with R, you need to first download and install the R software on your computer. Here are the steps to do so:

1. Go to the R project website at `https://www.r-project.org/`
2. Click on the "Download R" link in the middle of the page under "Getting Started".
3. Select a CRAN location (a mirror site) and click the corresponding link.
4. Click on the "Download R for (your OS)" link at the top of the page.
5. Click on the file containing the latest version of R under "Files."
6. Save the .exe file on your computer and run the installer.

Once you have installed R on your computer, you can use an interface to interact with it. There are several interfaces available, including RStudio, which is a popular and user-friendly interface. Here are the steps to install and use RStudio:

1. Go to the RStudio website at `https://www.rstudio.com/products/rstudio/download/`.
2. Under "Installers for Supported Platforms," click on the download link for your operating system (e.g., Windows, Mac, Linux).
3. Once the download is complete, run the installer and follow the prompts to install RStudio.
4. Once the installation is complete, open RStudio.
5. In RStudio, you will see several panels, including a console panel where you can type R commands and see their output.
6. To execute a command, simply type it in the console panel and press Enter.
7. You can also create and edit scripts in RStudio by going to File ¿ New File ¿ R Script.
8. Type your commands into the script editor, and then click the "Run" button to execute them.

4.3 Variables and Data Types

In R, a variable is a container for storing data values. Each variable has a name and a data type. R supports several data types, including:

- Numeric: used to store numerical data such as integers and decimals. Examples: 5, 3.14
- Integer: used to store integer values. Examples: 5L, -3L

- Character: used to store text data. Examples: "Hello", "R programming"
- Logical: used to store boolean values, i.e., TRUE or FALSE. Examples: TRUE, FALSE
- Factor: used to store categorical data. Examples: "red", "green", "blue"

Here's an example of creating variables with different data types in R:

```
# Numeric variable
x <- 5.5

# Integer variable
y <- 10L

# Character variable
z <- "Hello, world!"

# Logical variable
a <- TRUE

# Factor variable
b <- factor(c("male", "female", "male", "female"))
```

In this example, the variable x is of type numeric, y is of type integer, z is of type character, a is of type logical, and b is of type factor.

You can check the data type of a variable using the `class()` function, like this:

```
class(x)  # Output: "numeric"
class(y)  # Output: "integer"
class(z)  # Output: "character"
class(a)  # Output: "logical"
class(b)  # Output: "factor"
```

In R, variables are dynamically typed, which means that you can change their data type at any time by assigning a new value to them. For example:

```
x <- 5
class(x)  # Output: "integer"

x <- "hello"
class(x)  # Output: "character"
```

In this example, the variable x is first assigned the value 5, which makes it an integer type. However, when it is later assigned the value "hello", it becomes a character type instead.

4.4 Operators

Operators in R are symbols or keywords that are used to perform various mathematical, logical, or assignment operations on variables or values. Here are some commonly used operators in R:

Table 4.1: Operators in R

Category	Operators
Arithmetic	Addition (+), Subtraction (-), Multiplication (*), Division (/), Exponentiation (ˆ or **), Modulus (Remainder) (%)
Relational	Equal to (==), Not equal to (!= or ¡¿), Less than (¡), Less than or equal to (¡=), Greater than (¿), Greater than or equal to (¿=)
Logical	AND (&, &&), OR (—, ——), NOT (!)
Assignment	Assignment (¡- or =), Compound Assignment (+=, -=, *=, /=, ˆ=, %=)
Miscellaneous	Colon Operator (:), Membership Operator (%in%), Accessor Operators ($, @), Subset Operator ([])

Here are some examples of using operators in R: **Arithmetic operators:**

Arithmetic operators:

```
x <- 5
y <- 2
z <- x + y   # Output: 7
z <- x * y   # Output: 10
z <- x ^ y   # Output: 25
```

Relational operators:

```
a <- 7
b <- 4
a > b       # Output: TRUE
a == b      # Output: FALSE
```

Logical operators:

```
p <- TRUE
q <- FALSE
p & q       # Output: FALSE
p | q       # Output: TRUE
!p          # Output: FALSE
```

Assignment operators:

```
x <- 10
y <<- 20
z -> 30
x + y + z   # Output: 60
```

Miscellaneous operators:

```
# Colon Operator (:)
# Create a sequence from 1 to 10
sequence <- 1:10
print(sequence)

# Membership Operator (%in%)
# Check if a value exists in a vector
values <- c(2, 5, 8)
print(5 %in% values)  # Output: TRUE
print(7 %in% values)  # Output: FALSE

# Accessor Operators ($, @)
# Access elements of a list using the $ operator
person <- list(name = "John", age = 30, city = "New York")
print(person$name)  # Output: John
print(person$age)   # Output: 30

# Access elements of a data frame using the $ operator
# We can also use the @ operator to access elements of a S4 object
# For simplicity, let's create a simple data frame
df <- data.frame(name = c("Alice", "Bob", "Charlie"),
                 age = c(25, 30, 35))
print(df$name)      # Output: Alice Bob Charlie
print(df$age)       # Output: 25 30 35

# Subset Operator ([])
# Extract elements from a vector or data structure
vector <- c(10, 20, 30, 40, 50)
print(vector[2:4])  # Output: 20 30 40

# Extract rows and columns from a matrix or data frame
matrix <- matrix(1:9, nrow = 3)
print(matrix)
# Output:
#      [,1] [,2] [,3]
# [1,]    1    4    7
# [2,]    2    5    8
# [3,]    3    6    9
```

```
print(matrix[2, 3])  # Output: 8
print(matrix[1:2, ]) # Output: Rows 1 and 2
print(matrix[, 2:3]) # Output: Columns 2 and 3
```

4.5 Control Structures

if-else statements:

```
# Example 1: Determine if a number is positive or negative
num <- -3
if (num >= 0) {
  print("The number is positive")
} else {
  print("The number is negative")
}

# Example 2: Determine if a number is odd or even
num <- 7
if (num %% 2 == 0) {
  print("The number is even")
} else {
  print("The number is odd")
}
```

In the first example, we use an if-else statement to determine whether a given number is positive or negative. If the number is greater than or equal to zero, we print "The number is positive"; otherwise, we print "The number is negative". In the second example, we use an if-else statement to determine whether a given number is odd or even. We use the modulus operator (%%) to check if the remainder of the number divided by 2 is equal to 0.

switch:

```
# Example 1: Determine the type of a given variable
var <- 3.14
switch(class(var),
       "numeric" = print("The variable is numeric"),
       "character" = print("The variable is character"),
       "logical" = print("The variable is logical"))
```

In this example, we use the `switch()` function to determine the type of a given variable. Depending on the class of the variable `var`, different messages are printed.

For loop, while loop:

```
# Example 1: for loop
for (i in 1:5) {
```

```
  print(i)
}

# Example 2: while loop
i <- 1
while (i <= 5) {
  print(i)
  i <- i + 1
}
```

In the above examples, we use a `for` loop to print the numbers 1 to 5. The loop runs for each value of `i` in the sequence 1:5, and the value of `i` is printed on each iteration. In the second example, we use a `while` loop to print the numbers 1 to 5. The loop runs as long as the value of `i` is less than or equal to 5, and the value of `i` is incremented by 1 on each iteration.

4.6 R Objects

In R, an object is a data structure that holds data values and provides methods for manipulating those values. There are several types of objects in R, including:

- Arrays: used to store data values of multiple dimensions. An array can be of type numeric, character, logical, or complex.
- Matrices: used to store a two-dimensional table of data values of the same data type. A matrix can be of type numeric, character, logical, or complex.
- Vectors: used to store a sequence of data values of the same data type. A vector can be of type numeric, character, logical, or complex.
- Lists: used to store a collection of objects, which can be of any data type.
- Data frames: used to store tabular data in which each column can be of a different data type. A data frame is similar to a spreadsheet or a SQL table.

4.6.1 Creating Arrays

You can create arrays in R using the `array()` function. The function takes the data elements, dimensions (number of rows, columns, and depth), and optionally, dimension names as arguments.

```
# Create a 3-dimensional array
my_array <- array(1:24, dim = c(4, 3, 2))
print(my_array)
```

This will create a 4x3x2 array with elements from 1 to 24.

Accessing Elements

You can access elements of an array using indices for each dimension. In R, indexing starts from 1.

```
# Access an element
element <- my_array[2, 3, 1]
print(element)  # Output: 14
```

This will access the element in the second row, third column, and first depth of the array.

Operations on Arrays

Arrays support various arithmetic and linear algebra operations such as element-wise operations, array multiplication, transpose, and more.

```
# Element-wise addition
result_addition <- array1 + array2

# Array multiplication
result_multiplication <- array1 * array2

# Transpose of an array
transposed_array <- t(array1)
```

Here, `array1` and `array2` are assumed to be predefined arrays.

Functions for Arrays

R provides several functions to work with arrays efficiently. Some commonly used functions include:

- `dim()`: Returns the dimensions of an array.

- `apply()`: Apply a function over the margins of an array.

Examples of Functions

Here are examples demonstrating the usage of `dim()` and `apply()` functions:

```
# dim(): Returns dimensions
dimensions <- dim(my_array)
print(dimensions)

# apply(): Apply a function
# Example: Calculate column-wise sums
col_sums <- apply(my_array, c(1, 2), sum)
print(col_sums)
```

4.6.2 Matrices

In R, matrices are two-dimensional arrays that contain elements of the same data type. They are useful for storing and manipulating data in a tabular format.

Creating Matrices

You can create matrices in R using the `matrix()` function. The function takes the data elements, number of rows, and number of columns as arguments.

```
# Create a matrix
my_matrix <- matrix(c(1, 2, 3, 4, 5, 6), nrow = 3, ncol = 2)
print(my_matrix)
```

This will create a 3x2 matrix with elements from 1 to 6.

Accessing Elements

You can access elements of a matrix using row and column indices. In R, indexing starts from 1.

```
# Access an element
element <- my_matrix[1, 2]
print(element)  # Output: 2
```

This will access the element in the first row and second column of the matrix.

Operations on Matrices

Matrices support various arithmetic and linear algebra operations such as element-wise operations, matrix multiplication, transpose, and determinant calculation. Here, `matrix1` and `matrix2` are assumed to be predefined matrices.

```
# Element-wise addition
result_addition <- matrix1 + matrix2

# Matrix multiplication
result_multiplication <- matrix1 %*% t(matrix2)

# Transpose of a matrix
transposed_matrix <- t(matrix1)

# Determinant of a matrix
det_matrix <- det(matrix1)
```

Functions for Matrices

R provides several functions to work with matrices efficiently. Some commonly used functions include:

- `dim()`: Returns the dimensions (rows and columns) of a matrix.

- `rownames()` and `colnames()`: Retrieve or set row and column names.
- `apply()`: Apply a function to the rows or columns of a matrix.
- `rbind()` and `cbind()`: Combine matrices by rows or columns.

Examples of Functions

Here are examples demonstrating the usage of `dim()`, `rbind()`, `cbind()`, and `apply()` functions:

```
# dim(): Returns dimensions
dimensions <- dim(my_matrix)
print(dimensions)

# rbind(): Combine matrices by rows
matrix3 <- matrix(7:8, nrow = 1)
combined_matrix <- rbind(my_matrix, matrix3)
print(combined_matrix)

# cbind(): Combine matrices by columns
matrix4 <- matrix(9:10, nrow = 2)
combined_matrix <- cbind(my_matrix, matrix4)
print(combined_matrix)

# apply(): Apply a function
# Example: Calculate row-wise sums
row_sums <- apply(my_matrix, 1, sum)
print(row_sums)
```

Here's an example of creating and using some of these objects in R:

```
# Create a numeric vector
x <- c(1, 2, 3, 4, 5)

# Create a character vector
y <- c("apple", "banana", "orange")

# Create a matrix
m <- matrix(1:9, nrow = 3, ncol = 3)

# Create a data frame
df <- data.frame(name = c("Alice", "Bob", "Charlie"),
                 age = c(25, 30, 35),
                 married = c(TRUE, FALSE, TRUE))

# Create a list
l <- list(x, y, m, df)
```

```
# Accessing elements of an object
x[2]       # Output: 2
y[1]       # Output: "apple"
m[1, 2]    # Output: 4
df$name    # Output: "Alice", "Bob", "Charlie"
l[[3]]     # Output: 1 4 7 2 5 8 3 6 9
```

In this example, we create a numeric vector x, a character vector y, a matrix m, a data frame df, and a list l. We can access elements of these objects using the indexing operator [] for vectors and matrices, and the $ operator for data frames. We can access elements of a list using double square brackets [[ ]].

4.6.3 Vectors

In R, a vector is a one-dimensional array that can hold a sequence of data values of the same data type. There are four types of vectors in R: numeric, character, logical, and complex. Here are some examples of creating and working with vectors in R:

```
# Create a numeric vector
nums <- c(1, 2, 3, 4, 5)

# Create a character vector
chars <- c("apple", "banana", "orange")

# Create a logical vector
logicals <- c(TRUE, FALSE, TRUE)

# Create a complex vector
comps <- c(1+2i, 3+4i, 5+6i)

# Accessing elements of a vector
nums[2]      # Output: 2
chars[1]     # Output: "apple"
logicals[3]  # Output: TRUE
comps[2]     # Output: 3+4i

# Vector arithmetic
x <- c(1, 2, 3)
y <- c(4, 5, 6)
z <- x + y    # Output: 5 7 9
w <- x * y    # Output: 4 10 18

# Vector functions
mean(x)      # Output: 2
```

```
length(y)      # Output: 3
sum(z)         # Output: 21
```

In this example, we create four vectors: a numeric vector `nums`, a character vector `chars`, a logical vector `logicals`, and a complex vector `comps`. We access elements of these vectors using the indexing operator `[]`. We can perform arithmetic operations on vectors, and we can also use vector functions like `mean()`, `length()`, and `sum()`.

4.6.4 Lists

In R, a list is a data structure that can hold elements of different types, including other lists. It is a collection of objects (vectors, matrices, data frames, functions, etc.) with different lengths and data types. Here are some examples of creating and working with lists in R:

```
# Create a list
my_list <- list(name = "John", age = 30, hobbies = c("reading",
              "hiking"))

# Accessing elements of a list
my_list$name        # Output: "John"
my_list$age         # Output: 30
my_list$hobbies     # Output: "reading" "hiking"

# Adding elements to a list
my_list$gender <- "male"
my_list             # Output: $name [1] "John"
                    #          $age [1] 30
                    #          $hobbies [1] "reading" "hiking"
                    #          $gender [1] "male"

# Nested lists
nested_list <- list(a = c(1, 2, 3), b = list(x = "apple",
y = "banana"))
nested_list$a        # Output: 1 2 3
nested_list$b$x      # Output: "apple"

# List functions
length(my_list)      # Output: 4
names(my_list)       # Output: "name" "age" "hobbies" "gender"
```

In this example, we create a list `my_list` with three elements: `name`, `age`, and `hobbies`. We access elements of the list using the `$` operator. We add a new element to the list using the same operator. We also create a nested list `nested_list` that contains a vector and another list. We can get the length and names of a list using the `length()` and `names()` functions, respectively.

Table 4.2: Differences between Lists and Vectors

Lists	**Vectors**
Can contain elements of different data types	Must contain elements of the same data type
Elements can be of different lengths	All elements must be of the same length
Accessed using numeric indices or names	Accessed using numeric indices
Flexible and versatile	More restrictive
Commonly used for storing heterogeneous data structures	Commonly used for storing homogeneous data
Created using the `list()` function	Created using functions like `c()`, `numeric()`, etc.

Table 4.3: Differences between Arrays and Matrices

Arrays	**Matrices**
Can have more than two dimensions	Are two-dimensional
Elements can be of different data types	Elements are of the same data type
Accessed using multiple indices	Accessed using row and column indices
Created using the `array()` function	Created using the `matrix()` function
More general-purpose, can store multi-dimensional data	Specifically designed for linear algebra operations

4.6.5 Data Frames

Creating a Data Frame: We can create a data frame in R using the `data.frame()` function.

```
# create a data frame
df <- data.frame(
  name = c("John", "Mary", "Peter"),  age = c(25, 30, 35),
  salary = c(50000, 60000, 70000) )
```

Viewing Data Frame: We can use the `head()` function to view the top few rows of the data frame or use the `str()` function to view the structure of the data frame.

```
# view the top 6 rows of the data frame
head(df)

# view the structure of the data frame
str(df)
```

Accessing Data Frame Elements: We can use the $ operator to access the individual columns of the data frame, and the [ ] operator to access the individual elements, rows, and columns of the data frame.

```
# access the salary column
df$salary

# access the second row of the data frame
df[2,]

# access the age of the second row
df[2,"age"]
```

Adding Rows or Columns to Data Frame: We can add rows to the data frame using the `rbind()` function, and columns using the `cbind()` function.

```
# add a new row to the data frame
new_row <- data.frame(name = "Tom", age = 28, salary = 55000)
df <- rbind(df, new_row)

# add a new column to the data frame
gender <- c("Male", "Female", "Male", "Male")
df <- cbind(df, gender)
```

Filtering Data Frame: We can filter the data frame based on specific criteria using the `subset()` function.

```
# filter the data frame for rows where age is greater than 30
df_filtered <- subset(df, age > 30)
```

Merging Data Frames: We can merge two or more data frames into one using the `merge()` function.

```
# create another data frame
df2 <- data.frame(name = c("John", "Mary", "Peter"),
                  department = c("HR", "Sales", "IT"))

# merge the two data frames
df_merged <- merge(df, df2)
```

4.7 Factors in R

In R, factors are a data type used to represent categorical data. They are useful when you have a limited number of unique values that a variable can take. Factors in R are stored as integers, where each integer value has a corresponding label. Factors are especially useful for statistical modeling and data analysis tasks.

Creating Factors

```
# Creating a factor from a character vector
gender <- c("Male", "Female", "Male", "Female", "Male")
gender_factor <- factor(gender)

# Creating a factor with specified levels
temperature <- c("Low", "High", "Medium", "Low")
temperature_factor <- factor(temperature,
                              levels = c("Low", "Medium", "High"))
```

Working with Factors

- **Levels:** The `levels()` function returns the levels of a factor.
- **Summary:** The `summary()` function provides a summary of the factor, including the counts of each level.
- **Accessing and Modifying Levels:** You can access and modify levels of a factor using the `levels()` function.
- **Converting Factors to Numeric:** You can convert factors to numeric using `as.numeric()` function.
- **Converting Factors to Characters:** You can convert factors to character vectors using `as.character()`.
- **Manipulating Levels:** You can manipulate factor levels using functions like `reorder()` and `droplevels()`.

4.8 Functions

Built-in Functions: R has many built-in functions that can be used to perform various tasks. Some examples of built-in functions in R are `sum()`, `mean()`, `sd()`, `max()`, `min()`, etc. We can use these functions directly in R without defining them.

Defining Functions: We can define our own functions in R using the `function()` keyword. Here is an example of a simple function that takes two arguments and returns their sum:

```
# define a function
my_sum <- function(x, y){
  return(x + y)
}

# call the function
result <- my_sum(5, 10)
print(result)
```

Function Arguments: Functions in R can have one or more arguments. We can specify the default values for arguments, and we can also specify the argument names while calling the function. Here is an example:

```
# define a function with default argument values
my_power <- function(x, n = 2){
  return(x^n)
}

# call the function with named arguments
result1 <- my_power(x = 5)
result2 <- my_power(x = 5, n = 3)

print(result1)
print(result2)
```

Returning Values: Functions in R can return one or more values. We can use the `return()` keyword to specify the values to be returned. Here is an example:

```
# define a function that returns multiple values
my_stats <- function(x){
  mean_val <- mean(x)
  sd_val <- sd(x)

  return(list(mean_val, sd_val))
}

# call the function
result <- my_stats(c(1, 2, 3, 4, 5))

print(result[[1]])  # prints the mean value
print(result[[2]])  # prints the standard deviation value
```

Anonymous Functions: In R, we can also create anonymous functions using the `function()` keyword. Anonymous functions are also known as lambda functions or closures. They are useful when we want to apply a function to a subset of data or within another function. Here's an example of an anonymous function:

Recursive Functions: Recursive functions are functions that call themselves within their own code block. They are particularly useful when we need to perform a repetitive task that involves similar computations. In R, we can create recursive functions using the `if` statement or the `while` loop. Here's an example of a simple recursive function in R that calculates the factorial of a given number:

In the above example, the `factorial()` function takes a single argument `n`, which is the number whose factorial we want to compute. The `if` statement

Table 4.4: R Code for Calculating Factorial

```
# Recursive function for computing factorial of a number
factorial <- function(n) {
  if (n == 1) {
    return(1)
  } else {
    return(n * factorial(n - 1))
  }
}

# Call the function with a sample value
factorial(5)
```

checks if `n` is equal to 1. If it is, the function returns 1. Otherwise, it calls itself with the argument `n - 1` and multiplies the result with `n`.

4.9 Debugging and Simulation in R

Debugging in R

Debugging is the process of finding and fixing errors in code. R provides several tools for debugging code:

- `browser()`: This function sets a breakpoint at a specific line of code, causing R to enter debugging mode when that line is executed. Once in debugging mode, you can step through the code line by line to identify the error.

```
myfun <- function(x, y) {
   z <- x + y
   browser() # pause execution and enter debugging mode
   if (z > 10) {
      print("Greater than 10")
   } else {
      print("Less than or equal to 10")
   }
}
```

- `traceback()`: This function shows the call stack for the current execution environment. It can be used to identify where an error occurred and which functions were called to reach that point.

```
myfun <- function(x, y) {
   z <- x + y
   if (z > 10) {
      print("Greater than 10")
   } else {
      stop("Error: Less than or equal to 10")
      # stop execution and print error message
   }
}
myfun(5, 3)
traceback()
```

- `debug()`: This function sets a breakpoint at the beginning of a specified function. When the function is called, R enters debugging mode and allows you to step through the function to identify the error.

- `trace()`: This function allows you to add additional code to a function that is executed each time the function is called. This can be useful for debugging purposes, as you can print out variable values or other information at each step in the function.

Simulation in R

Simulation involves generating data sets that mimic the behavior of real-world data sets. R provides several functions for simulating data:

- `rnorm()`: This function generates a random sample from a normal distribution with a specified mean and standard deviation.

- `runif()`: This function generates a random sample from a uniform distribution between specified minimum and maximum values.

- `rpois()`: This function generates a random sample from a Poisson distribution with a specified mean.

- `rbinom()`: This function generates a random sample from a binomial distribution with specified number of trials and probability of success.

- `rexp()`: This function generates a random sample from an exponential distribution with a specified rate parameter.

Simulated data can be used for a variety of purposes, including testing statistical models and evaluating the performance of algorithms.

4.10 Introduction to Data Prepossessing in R

Data preprocessing is essential to ensure the quality and reliability of the data before performing any analysis or building predictive models. Here's an overview of common data preprocessing tasks and techniques in R:

1. **Data Loading**: The first step in data preprocessing is loading the data into R. R provides functions like `read.csv()`, `read.table()`, `read.xlsx()`, etc., to import data from various file formats such as CSV, text, Excel, etc.

2. **Exploratory Data Analysis (EDA)**: EDA encompasses the process of delving into a dataset to grasp its underlying structure, attributes, and inter-variable relationships. In R, EDA is facilitated by functions such as `str()`, `summary()`, `head()`, `tail()`, alongside visualization techniques like histograms, boxplots, scatter plots, among others.

3. **Handling Missing Values**: Missing values are common in real-world datasets and can adversely affect analysis and modeling. R provides functions like `is.na()`, `na.omit()`, `complete.cases()`, and packages like `naniar` for identifying and handling missing values through imputation or deletion.

4. **Dealing with Outliers**: Outliers represent data points that deviate notably from the rest of the observations within a dataset. In R, a range of statistical methodologies and visualization aids such as boxplots, scatter plots, and robust techniques like Z-score, IQR, etc., are available to identify and address outliers effectively.

5. **Data Transformation**: Data transformation pertains to the process of converting data into a format conducive to analysis. This encompasses tasks such as scaling, normalization, categorical variable encoding, feature engineering, and more. In R, a suite of functions including `scale()`, `log()`, `sqrt()`, `factor()`, among others, facilitates data transformation tasks efficiently.

6. **Feature Selection and Dimensionality Reduction**: Feature selection involves selecting the most relevant features or variables for analysis or modeling. Dimensionality reduction techniques like Principal Component Analysis (PCA), Singular Value Decomposition (SVD), etc., are used to reduce the number of features while retaining important information.

7. **Data Splitting**: Preceding modeling, datasets are typically partitioned into training and testing subsets to assess model performance. R offers functionalities such as `sample()`, `createDataPartition()` from the caret package, among others, facilitating the division of data into training and testing sets.

8. **Data Standardization and Normalization**: Standardization and normalization techniques aim to scale numerical features to a consistent scale, thereby improving model performance and convergence. In R, utilities such as `scale()` and various min-max normalization techniques enable effective implementation of standardization and normalization procedures.

R code for data preprocessing

The code manipulates and prepares the Iris dataset using R. It loads necessary libraries and the dataset, displays initial rows, summarizes the data, and checks for missing values. A boxplot detects outliers in ‘Sepal.Length‘, and rows with missing values are removed. Numeric variables are standardized. A correlation matrix identifies the two most correlated features with the target variable ‘Species‘. The final dataset includes these features and the target, displaying the first few rows.

Table 4.5: R Code for Data Preprocessing

```
# Load necessary libraries
library(datasets)  # for accessing datasets
library(dplyr)     # for data manipulation
# Load the Iris dataset
data(iris)
# Display the first few rows of the dataset
head(iris)
# Summary of the dataset
summary(iris)
# Check for missing values
colSums(is.na(iris))
# Create boxplot for each numeric variable to detect outliers
# Here, we use Sepal.Length as an example
boxplot(iris$Sepal.Length)
# Handle missing values (if any)
# For demonstration, let's remove rows with missing values
clean_data <- na.omit(iris)
# Data transformation (if needed)
# For demonstration, let's standardize the numeric variables
standardized_data <- scale(clean_data[, 1:4])
# Feature selection
# let's select the two most important features using correlation
# Compute the correlation matrix
cor_matrix <- cor(clean_data[, 1:4])
# Find the absolute correlation values for each feature
cor_values <- apply(cor_matrix, 2, function(x) abs(x))
# Select  2 features with the highest correlation with the target
selected_features <-
names(sort(cor_values[, "Species"], decreasing = TRUE)[1:2])
# Select the columns with the selected features
selected_data <- clean_data[, c(selected_features, "Species")]
# Display the first few rows of the selected dataset
head(selected_data)
```

4.11 Experiments

1. **Find the Sum, Mean, and Product of the Vector**

```
# Example vector
vector <- c(1, 2, 3, 4, 5)

# Sum of the vector
vector_sum <- sum(vector)
print(paste("Sum of the vector:", vector_sum))

# Mean of the vector
vector_mean <- mean(vector)
print(paste("Mean of the vector:", vector_mean))

# Product of the vector
vector_product <- prod(vector)
print(paste("Product of the vector:", vector_product))
```

2. **Check the given number is even or odd**

```
check_even_odd <- function(number) {
  if (number %% 2 == 0) {
    return("even")
  } else {
    return("odd")
  }
}

# Example usage
input_number <- 7  # Change this to the number you want to check
result <- check_even_odd(input_number)
print(paste("The number", input_number, "is", result))
```

3. **Generate the Multiplication of Table**

```
# Define the size of the multiplication table
size <- 10

# Generate the multiplication table
multiplication_table <- outer(1:size, 1:size, "*")

# Print the multiplication table
print(multiplication_table)
```

4. **Find the factorial of the given number**

```
% Example number
Let's calculate the factorial of \( 5 \).

% Calculate factorial using the factorial() function
 factorial_5 <- factorial(5)
```

5. **Determine the given number is prime or not**

```
is_prime <- function(n) {
  if (n <= 1) {
    return(FALSE)
  }
  for (i in 2:(sqrt(n))) {
    if (n %% i == 0) {
      return(FALSE)
    }
  }
  return(TRUE)
}

# Example usage
number <- 29  # Change this to the number you want to check
if (is_prime(number)) {
  print(paste(number, "is a prime number."))
} else {
  print(paste(number, "is not a prime number."))
}
```

6. **Print Fibonacci Series**

```
fibonacci <- function(n) {
  if (n <= 0) {
    return(NULL)
  } else if (n == 1) {
    return(0)
  } else if (n == 2) {
    return(c(0, 1))
  } else {
    fib_series <- numeric(n)
    fib_series[1:2] <- c(0, 1)
    for (i in 3:n) {
      fib_series[i] <- fib_series[i - 1] + fib_series[i - 2]
```

```
    }
    return(fib_series)
  }
}

# Example usage
num_terms <- 10
fib_series <- fibonacci(num_terms)
print(fib_series)
```

7. **Convert the temperature from Celsius to Fahrenheit**

```
celsius_to_fahrenheit <- function(celsius) {
  return((celsius * 9/5) + 32)
}

# Example usage
celsius_temp <- 25
fahrenheit_temp <- celsius_to_fahrenheit(celsius_temp)
print(paste(celsius_temp, "degrees Celsius is equal to",
                        fahrenheit_temp, "degrees Fahrenheit."))
```

8. **Count the number of vowels in a string**

```
count_vowels <- function(string) {
  vowels <- c("a", "e", "i", "o", "u", "A", "E", "I", "O", "U")
  count <- 0
  for (char in strsplit(string, "")[[1]]) {
    if (char %in% vowels) {
      count <- count + 1
    }
  }
  return(count)
}

# Example usage
input_string <- "Hello, World!"
num_vowels <- count_vowels(input_string)
print(paste("Number of vowels in the string:", num_vowels))
```

9. **Perform various Matrix Operations**

```
    # Define two matrices
```

```
mat1 <- matrix(1:9, nrow = 3, byrow = TRUE)
mat2 <- matrix(9:1, nrow = 3, byrow = TRUE)

# Display the matrices
print("Matrix 1:")
print(mat1)
print("Matrix 2:")
print(mat2)

# Addition
print("Matrix Addition:")
print(mat1 + mat2)

# Subtraction
print("Matrix Subtraction:")
print(mat1 - mat2)

# Multiplication (element-wise)
print("Element-wise Multiplication:")
print(mat1 * mat2)

# Division (element-wise)
print("Element-wise Division:")
print(mat1 / mat2)

# Matrix Multiplication
print("Matrix Multiplication:")
print(mat1 %*% t(mat2))

# Transpose
print("Transpose of Matrix 1:")
print(t(mat1))

# Inverse (requires non-singular square matrix)
# We'll use the solve function to calculate the inverse
if (det(mat1) != 0) {  # Check if matrix is non-singular
  print("Inverse of Matrix 1:")
  print(solve(mat1))
} else {
  print("Matrix 1 is singular, inverse does not exist.")
}

# Determinant (requires square matrix)
# We'll use the det function to calculate the determinant
if (nrow(mat1) == ncol(mat1)) {  # Check if matrix is square
```

```
    print("Determinant of Matrix 1:")
    print(det(mat1))
  } else {
    print("Matrix 1 is not square, determinant does not exist.")
  }

  # Eigenvalues and Eigenvectors (requires square matrix)
  # use eigen() to calculate eigenvalues, eigenvectors
  if (nrow(mat1) == ncol(mat1)) {
   # Check if matrix is square
    print("Eigenvalues of Matrix 1:")
    print(eigen(mat1)$values)
    print("Eigenvectors of Matrix 1:")
    print(eigen(mat1)$vectors)
  } else {
    print("eigenvalues and eigenvectors do not exist.")
  }
```

10. **Descriptive Statistics**

```
# load the package
library(mlbench)

# load the dataset
data(PimaIndiansDiabetes)

# display first 20 rows of data
head(PimaIndiansDiabetes, n=20)

# display the dimensions of the dataset
dim(PimaIndiansDiabetes)

# distribution of class variable
y <- PimaIndiansDiabetes$diabetes
cbind(freq=table(y), percentage=prop.table(table(y))*100)

# summarize the dataset
summary(PimaIndiansDiabetes)

# calculate standard deviation for all attributes
sapply(PimaIndiansDiabetes[,1:8], sd)

skew <- apply(PimaIndiansDiabetes[,1:8], 2, skewness)
#display skewness, larger/smaller deviations from 0 show more skew
```

```
print(skew)

# calculate a correlation matrix for numeric variables
correlations <- cor(PimaIndiansDiabetes[,1:8])
# display the correlation matrix
print(correlations)
```

11. **Data Visualization**

```
# Load necessary packages
library(ggplot2)
library(gridExtra)

# Load the Iris dataset
data(iris)

# Univariate plots
# Histograms
hist_plots <- lapply(names(iris)[-5],
function(x) ggplot(iris,aes_string(x)) +
geom_histogram(fill = "skyblue", color = "black",
bins = 10) +  labs(title = paste("Histogram of", x),
                      x = x, y = "Frequency"))

# Density plots
density_plots <- lapply(names(iris)[-5],
function(x) ggplot(iris,aes_string(x)) +
geom_density(fill = "skyblue", color = "black") +
  labs(title = paste("Density Plot of", x),
  x = x, y = "Density"))

# Box and whisker plots
box_plots <- lapply(names(iris)[-5],
function(x) ggplot(iris,
aes(x = Species, y = .data[[x]])) +
geom_boxplot(fill = "skyblue",
color = "black") +
labs(title = paste("Boxplot of", x),
             x = "Species", y = x))

# Bar plots
bar_plots <- lapply(names(iris)[-5],
function(x) ggplot(iris,
aes_string(x)) +  geom_bar(fill = "skyblue",
color = "black", alpha = 0.7) +
```

```
labs(title = paste("Bar Plot of", x),
  x = x, y = "Count") +
  theme(axis.text.x = element_text(angle = 45, hjust = 1)))

# Multivariate plots
# Correlation plot
correlation_plot <- ggplot(iris, aes(x = Sepal.Length,
y = Sepal.Width,color = Species)) +
  geom_point() +
  labs(title = "Correlation Plot",
  x = "Sepal Length",  y = "Sepal Width")

# Scatterplot matrix
scatterplot_matrix <- ggplot(iris, aes(x = Sepal.Length,
y = Sepal.Width, color = Species)) +  geom_point() +
facet_grid(Species ~ .) +  labs(title = "Scatterplot Matrix",
x = "Sepal Length",
  y = "Sepal Width")

# Scatterplot matrix by class
scatterplot_matrix_class <- ggplot(iris, aes(x = Sepal.Length,
y = Sepal.Width)) +  geom_point() +  facet_wrap(~ Species) +
  labs(title = "Scatterplot Matrix by Class", x = "Sepal Length",
  y = "Sepal Width")

# Density by class
density_by_class <- ggplot(iris,
    aes(x = Sepal.Length, fill = Species))
+  geom_density(alpha = 0.5) +
  labs(title = "Density by Class", x = "Sepal Length")

# Box and whisker plots by class
box_plots_by_class <- ggplot(iris,
  aes(x = Species, y = Sepal.Length)) +
  geom_boxplot(fill = "skyblue", color = "black") +
  labs(title = "Boxplot by Class",
  x = "Species", y = "Sepal Length")

# Combine plots
univariate_plots <- grid.arrange(grobs =
  list(hist_plots, density_plots,
box_plots, bar_plots), ncol = 4)

multivariate_plots <- grid.arrange(correlation_plot,
scatterplot_matrix, scatterplot_matrix_class,density_by_class,
```

```
box_plots_by_class, ncol = 2)

# Display plots
print(univariate_plots)
print(multivariate_plots)
```

4.12 Exercises

4.12.1 Short and Long Answer Questions

1. Explain the concept of data frames in R and provide an example of how they are used in data analysis.

2. Describe the process of installing R packages and loading them into your R session.

3. What are vectors in R? Discuss the different types of vectors and provide examples.

4. Explain the difference between arithmetic, logical, and matrix operations in R with suitable examples.

5. Discuss the importance of control structures in programming and how they are implemented in R.

6. Write a function in R called "calculate_mean" that calculates the mean of a numeric vector passed as an argument.

7. What is debugging in R? Describe some common debugging techniques used in R programming.

8. Discuss the concept of hypothesis testing and provide an example of how it is applied in data analysis.

9. Explain the purpose of simulation in R and provide an example scenario where simulation is useful.

10. How do you read data from relational databases like MySQL into R? Describe the necessary steps and R packages involved.

11. Write R code to read a CSV file named "data.csv" into a data frame and display its first few rows.

12. Create a vector containing integers from 1 to 10 and calculate the mean, median, and standard deviation of the vector.

13. Generate a matrix of dimensions 3x3 filled with random numbers between 1 and 10. Calculate the sum of each row and each column.

14. Write a function in R called "fibonacci" that takes an integer parameter "n" and returns the nth Fibonacci number.

15. Create a scatter plot using the "mtcars" dataset in R, with miles per gallon (mpg) on the x-axis and horsepower (hp) on the y-axis.

16. Perform a linear regression analysis using the "mtcars" dataset to predict miles per gallon (mpg) based on horsepower (hp).

17. Implement a logistic regression model using the "iris" dataset to predict species (setosa, versicolor, virginica) based on sepal length and width.

18. Write R code to create a histogram of the "Sepal.Length" variable from the "iris" dataset, with 20 bins.

19. Use the "ggplot2" package to create a bar plot showing the count of each species in the "iris" dataset.

20. Calculate the correlation matrix for the variables "Sepal.Length", "Sepal.Width", "Petal.Length," and "Petal.Width" in the "iris" dataset.

4.12.2 Fill in the Blanks

1. In R programming, a vector can contain elements of the same ______.

2. The function used to install packages in R is `install.packages(______)`.

3. Logical operators in R are used to perform ______ operations.

4. A data frame in R is similar to a ______ in a database.

5. The correct syntax to define a function in R is `function_name` ______ {}.

6. In R, the `for` loop is used for ______ tasks.

7. Debugging in R involves identifying and fixing ______ in the code.

8. The `runif()` function in R is used to generate ______ random numbers.

9. The `apply()` function in R is used to apply a function to ______ of an array.

10. In R, the `merge()` function is used to combine ______ data frames.

4.12.3 Multiple Choice Questions

1. What is R Programming primarily used for?
   A) Web development
   B) Data analysis and statistical computing
   C) Mobile app development
   D) Game development

2. Which of the following is the correct way to install packages in R?
   A) install.packages(”package_name”)
   B) use.package(”package_name”)
   C) add.package(”package_name”)
   D) load.package(”package_name”)

3. What is the function of the ’c()’ function in R?
   A) Concatenation
   B) Calculation
   C) Conditional statement
   D) Control structure

4. What does the ’data.frame()’ function do in R?
   A) Creates a list of data frames
   B) Creates a matrix
   C) Creates a data frame
   D) Creates a vector

5. In R, what does the ’typeof()’ function do?
   A) Returns the storage mode of an object
   B) Checks the type of variable
   C) Returns the data type of an object
   D) Converts variables to a specified type

6. Which operator is used for exponentiation in R?
   A) ^
   B) *
   C) /
   D) %

7. What is the purpose of logical operators in R?
   A) To perform arithmetic operations
   B) To perform comparisons
   C) To create data frames
   D) To define functions

8. What is the correct syntax for defining a function in R?
   A) def function_name(parameters):
   B) function_name(parameters) { }
   C) function_name ¡- function(parameters) { }
   D) function function_name(parameters) { }

9. Which control structure is used for iterative tasks in R?
   A) if-else
   B) switch
   C) for loop
   D) while loop

10. What does the 'debug()' function do in R?
   A) Executes the code
   B) Steps through the code line by line for debugging
   C) Stops the execution of code
   D) Prints output

11. Which function is used to generate random numbers in R?
   A) rand()
   B) random()
   C) rnorm()
   D) random_numbers()

12. How do you access the help documentation for a specific function in R?
   A) help()
   B) get_help()
   C) ?function_name
   D) man()

13. Which operator is used to subset data in R?
   A) .
   B) :
   C) %in%
   D) $

14. What is the purpose of the 'apply()' function in R?
   A) Applies a function over margins of an array
   B) Applies a function to each element of a vector
   C) Applies a function to a data frame
   D) Applies a function to a matrix

15. How do you convert a factor to a character in R?
   A) as.character()
   B) to.character()
   C) convert.character()
   D) as.character.factor()

16. Which function is used to remove missing values from a dataset in R?
   A) removeNA()
   B) na.omit()
   C) removeMissing()
   D) removeNull()

17. In R, what is the purpose of the 'subset()' function?
    A) To create a subset of data based on a condition
    B) To remove a subset of data from a data frame
    C) To select specific columns from a data frame
    D) To split a data frame into smaller data frames

18. What is the purpose of the 'merge()' function in R?
    A) To combine two or more vectors
    B) To merge two or more data frames
    C) To merge two or more lists
    D) To perform matrix multiplication

19. How do you create a matrix in R?
    A) create.matrix()
    B) matrix()
    C) make.matrix()
    D) generate.matrix()

Chapter 5

Classification and Clustering

5.1 Classification

Classification is the process of finding a model (or function) that describes and distinguishes data classes or concepts. The model is derived based on the analysis of a set of training data, where the class labels are known. The model is then used to predict the class label of objects for which the label is unknown.

1. **Model Construction:** Build a model for predetermined classes.
2. **Model Usage:** Classify unknown data samples.

1. Model Construction: Describing a Set of Predetermined Classes

- Each data sample is assumed to belong to a predefined class, as determined by the class label attribute.
- Use a training dataset for model construction.
- The model is represented as classification rules, decision trees, or mathematical formulas.

2. Model Usage: For Classifying Future or Unknown Objects

- Estimate accuracy of the model.
- The known label of a test sample is compared with the classified result from the model.
- Test accuracy rate is the percentage of test set samples that are correctly classified by the model.

- Test set is independent of the training set but from the same probability distribution.

Construction and evaluation of a classifier require partitioning labeled data into a training set and a test set. Holdout, random sampling, cross-validation, and bootstrapping are typical methods used for such partitioning.

Applications of Classification Document categorization, Credit approval, Target marketing, Medical diagnosis, Treatment effectiveness analysis.

5.2 Classifier Performance Metrics

Classifier performance metrics are used to evaluate the effectiveness of a classification model. One of the key tools for evaluating classifier performance is the **confusion matrix**.

5.2.1 Confusion Matrix

A confusion matrix is a table that is often used to describe the performance of a classification model on a set of test data for which the true values are known. It helps to visualize the performance of an algorithm by presenting the actual and predicted classifications.

Table 5.1: Confusion Matrix

		Predicted	
		Positive	**Negative**
Actual	**Positive**	TP	FN
	Negative	FP	TN

True Positives (TP): The cases in which the model correctly predicts the positive class.
False Positives (FP): The cases in which the model incorrectly predicts the positive class.
True Negatives (TN): The cases in which the model correctly predicts the negative class.
False Negatives (FN): The cases in which the model incorrectly predicts the negative class.

Table of Classifier Performance Metrics

Table 5.2: Classifier Performance Metrics and Formulas

Metric	Formula
Accuracy	$\frac{TP+TN}{TP+TN+FP+FN}$
Error Rate	$\frac{FP+FN}{TP+TN+FP+FN}$
Precision	$\frac{TP}{TP+FP}$
Recall (Sensitivity)	$\frac{TP}{TP+FN}$
Specificity	$\frac{TN}{TN+FP}$
F1 Score	$2 \times \frac{\text{Precision} \times \text{Recall}}{\text{Precision} + \text{Recall}}$

5.2.2 Numerical Example

	Predicted Positive	**Predicted Negative**
Actual Positive	150 (TP)	20 (FN)
Actual Negative	30 (FP)	800 (TN)

$$\begin{aligned}
\text{Sensitivity (Recall)} &= \frac{\text{TP}}{\text{TP}+\text{FN}} = \frac{150}{150+20} = 0.882 \\
\text{Specificity} &= \frac{\text{TN}}{\text{TN}+\text{FP}} = \frac{800}{800+30} = 0.964 \\
\text{Precision} &= \frac{\text{TP}}{\text{TP}+\text{FP}} = \frac{150}{150+30} = 0.833 \\
\text{NPV} &= \frac{\text{TN}}{\text{TN}+\text{FN}} = \frac{800}{800+20} = 0.976 \\
\text{Accuracy} &= \frac{\text{TP}+\text{TN}}{\text{TP}+\text{TN}+\text{FP}+\text{FN}} = \frac{150+800}{150+800+30+20} = 0.961
\end{aligned}$$

The overall accuracy of the classification model is 0.961 or 96.1%.

Sensitivity (Recall) measures the proportion of actual positive cases that were correctly identified by the model. In this case, it tells us that the model correctly identified 88.2% of the actual positive cases.

Precision indicates the proportion of predicted positive cases that were actually positive. Here, the model correctly identified 83.3% of the predicted positive cases.

With only 20 False Negatives out of 170 actual positive cases, the model appears to be performing relatively well in minimizing False Negatives.

The False Positive Rate is not explicitly computed in this example, but it can be calculated as $\text{FPR} = \frac{\text{FP}}{\text{FP+TN}}$.

5.2.3 Receiver Operating Characteristic (ROC) Curve

The Receiver Operating Characteristic (ROC) curve is a graphical representation used to evaluate the performance of a binary classifier system. It illustrates the trade-off between the true positive rate (TPR) and the false positive rate (FPR) as the discrimination threshold is varied.

The ROC curve plots the True Positive Rate (Sensitivity) against the False Positive Rate (1 - Specificity) for different threshold values.

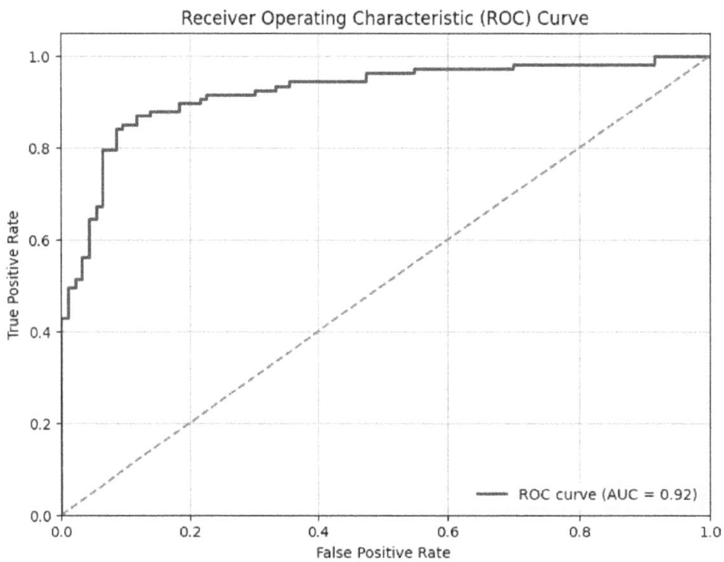

Figure 5.1: Receiver Operating Characteristic (ROC) Curve

In Figure 5.1, the diagonal line represents a random classifier, while the curve represents the classifier's performance. A perfect classifier would have a curve passing through the upper left corner (0, 1) of the graph, indicating high TPR and low FPR.

The area under the ROC curve (AUC) is a common metric used to quantify the performance of a classifier. AUC close to 1 indicates excellent performance, while AUC close to 0.5 suggests poor performance similar to a random classifier.

5.3 Ensemble Methods

Ensemble methods are machine learning techniques that combine the predictions of multiple base models to produce a final prediction. The idea behind ensemble methods is to leverage the wisdom of crowds, where aggregating the predictions of multiple models often results in better performance than any individual model alone. Ensemble methods are widely used in practice and have been shown to improve predictive accuracy across various domains.

5.3.1 Overview of Ensemble Methods

Ensemble methods work by training multiple base models independently and then combining their predictions in various ways to produce a final prediction. The diversity among the base models is crucial for the success of ensemble methods. If the base models are diverse and make different errors, the ensemble can correct individual mistakes and make more accurate predictions.

5.3.2 Common Ensemble Methods

1. **Bagging (Bootstrap Aggregating):**
    - Bagging involves training multiple base models (often decision trees) on different subsets of the training data, sampled with replacement (bootstrap sampling).
    - The final prediction is typically obtained by averaging the predictions of all base models for regression tasks or by taking a majority vote for classification tasks.
    - Random Forest is a popular ensemble method based on bagging, where decision trees are the base models.
2. **Boosting:**
    - Boosting focuses on sequentially training base models where each subsequent model corrects the errors made by the previous ones.
    - Models are trained iteratively, and each new model pays more attention to instances that were misclassified by the previous models.
    - Gradient Boosting Machines (GBM), AdaBoost, and XGBoost are common boosting algorithms widely used in practice.
3. **Stacking (Stacked Generalization):**
    - Stacking combines the predictions of multiple base models by training a meta-model (or blender) on their predictions.
    - Base models make predictions on the same dataset, and the meta-model learns to combine these predictions to produce the final output.

- Stacking allows for more complex relationships among base model predictions and often leads to improved performance.

4. **Voting Classifiers/Regression:**

   - Voting methods combine the predictions of multiple base models by taking a simple average (for regression) or a majority vote (for classification).
   - Hard voting involves combining the class labels predicted by individual models, while soft voting averages the predicted probabilities.
   - Voting classifiers/regressors are straightforward to implement and can achieve good performance, especially when the base models are diverse.

5.3.3 Advantages of Ensemble Methods

- **Improved Performance:** Ensemble methods often outperform individual models, especially when base models are diverse.
- **Robustness:** Ensembles are more robust to overfitting compared to individual models, especially when using bagging or boosting.
- **Handles Complexity:** Ensemble methods can capture complex patterns in data by combining the strengths of multiple models.
- **Versatility:** Ensemble methods can be applied to a wide range of machine learning tasks, including classification, regression, and clustering.

5.4 Logistic Regression in R Programming

Logistic regression in R is a classification algorithm used to find the probability of event success and event failure. It is employed when the dependent variable is binary (0/1, True/False, Yes/No) in nature. The logistic regression model is based on the sigmoid function, where the output is a probability ranging from 0 to 1, and the input can vary from negative to positive infinity.

5.4.1 Theory of Logistic Regression

Logistic regression is also known as a generalized linear model and is used as a classification technique to predict a qualitative response. The logistic regression model can be represented by the following equation:

$$p = \frac{1}{1 + e^{-(b_0+b_1x_1+b_2x_2+\dots)}}$$

where p is the probability of the characteristic of interest, and $b_0, b_1, b_2, \dots$ are the coefficients to be estimated based on the available training data.

The odds ratio, defined as the probability of success compared to the probability of failure, is a key representation of logistic regression coefficients and can take values between 0 and infinity. An odds ratio of 1 indicates that the probability of success is equal to the probability of failure.

The logit function, chosen as the link function, ensures that the logistic regression model is linearly related to the independent variables. It is represented as:

$$\text{logit}(p) = \ln\left(\frac{p}{1-p}\right) = b_0 + b_1x_1 + b_2x_2 + \ldots$$

where the logit is also known as the log of odds.

5.4.2 Implementation in R

In R, logistic regression can be implemented using the `glm()` function, which stands for generalized linear model. Here's an example of how to implement logistic regression in R:

```
# Load the dataset
data <- read.csv("data.csv")

# Fit the logistic regression model
model <- glm(outcome ~ predictor1 + predictor2,
                    data = data, family = binomial)

# Print the summary of the model
summary(model)
```

In the example above, the dataset is loaded using the `read.csv()` function, and the logistic regression model is fitted using the `glm()` function with the `family` argument set to `binomial` to indicate a binomial logistic regression model.

The summary of the model provides information such as coefficients, standard errors, p-values, and goodness-of-fit statistics.

It's important to check the assumptions of the model before interpreting the results, as logistic regression assumes a linear relationship between predictors and the log-odds of the outcome.

5.5 K-Nearest Neighbors (KNN) Algorithm

K-Nearest Neighbors (KNN) stands as a straightforward yet potent algorithm utilized for both classification and regression assignments. As a non-parametric and instance-based learning method, KNN determines predictions by gauging the resemblance between a new sample and the prevailing training examples.

Here's how the KNN algorithm works:

1. Choose the number of neighbors (k) to consider.

2. Calculate the distance between the new sample and each of the training examples.

3. Select the k training examples with the smallest distance to the new sample.

4. For classification tasks, assign the class label that is most common among the k nearest neighbors to the new sample. For regression tasks, assign the average value of the k nearest neighbors to the new sample.

5.5.1 K-Nearest Neighbors Implementation in R

In R, you can use the `knn()` function from the `class` package to implement the KNN algorithm. Here's an example of how to use KNN for classification:

```
# Load the iris dataset
data(iris)

# Split the data into training and testing sets
trainIndex <- sample(1:nrow(iris), 0.7*nrow(iris))
trainData <- iris[trainIndex, ]
testData <- iris[-trainIndex, ]

# Fit the KNN model
library(class)
k <- 3
knnModel <- knn(train = trainData[,1:4],
                test = testData[,1:4],
                cl = trainData[,5],
                k = k)

# Print the accuracy of the model
accuracy <- sum(knnModel == testData[,5])/nrow(testData)
cat("Accuracy:", round(accuracy, 2))
```

In the example above, we first load the iris dataset and split it into training and testing sets. We then use the `knn()` function to fit the KNN model to the training data and make predictions on the testing data. The k parameter is set to 3, which means we consider the 3 nearest neighbors when making predictions.

Finally, we calculate the accuracy of the model by comparing the predicted class labels to the actual class labels in the testing data. The output of the script will be the accuracy of the model, which is the proportion of correctly classified samples in the testing data.

5.6 Introduction to Clustering

5.6.1 Introduction to Clustering

Clustering is a fundamental task in unsupervised machine learning used to group similar data points together based on certain characteristics. It involves organizing unlabeled data into groups or clusters, where data points within the same cluster are more similar to each other than to those in other clusters.

Definition: Clustering is the process of dividing a set of data points into subsets, or clusters, so that data points in the same cluster are more similar to each other than to those in other clusters.

Difference from Classification: Clustering and classification are both machine learning techniques, but they differ in their objectives and approaches. While clustering aims to group similar data points together without prior knowledge of class labels, classification assigns predefined labels to data points based on their features and attributes.

Different Methods to Form Clusters: The process of forming clusters involves various methods, each with its own characteristics and applications.

- **K-Means:** Partitioning data into K clusters based on centroids.
- **Hierarchical:** Agglomerative or divisive approach to form clusters hierarchically.
- **DBSCAN:** Density-based clustering for identifying clusters in varying densities.
- **Mean Shift:** Iterative algorithm for finding dense regions in data.
- **Gaussian Mixture Models:** Probabilistic model assuming data points are generated from a mixture of Gaussian distributions.

Applications of Clustering: Clustering techniques find applications across various domains such as marketing, biology, finance, and computer vision, among others.

- **Customer Segmentation:** Grouping customers based on their purchasing behavior or demographic information.
- **Document Clustering:** Organizing documents into clusters based on their content or topics.
- **Image Segmentation:** Partitioning images into meaningful regions or objects.
- **Anomaly Detection:** Identifying unusual patterns or outliers in data.
- **Market Basket Analysis:** Analyzing purchase patterns to identify associations between products.

5.6.2 K-Means Algorithm

K-Means is a popular unsupervised machine learning algorithm used for clustering tasks. It works by partitioning the data into K clusters based on the similarity of the data points.

Here's how the K-Means algorithm works:

1. Choose the number of clusters (K) to form.
2. Initialize K cluster centroids randomly.
3. Assign each data point to the nearest centroid based on the Euclidean distance between the data point and the centroid.
4. Update the centroid of each cluster by computing the mean of all data points assigned to that cluster.
5. Repeat steps 3-4 until the centroids no longer change or a maximum number of iterations is reached.

5.6.3 Numerical Example

Cluster the points A1 $(2, 10)$, A2 $(2, 5)$, A3 $(8, 4)$, B1 $(5, 8)$, B2 $(7, 5)$, B3 $(6, 4)$, C1 $(1, 2)$, and C2 $(4, 9)$ into three clusters using the k-means algorithm. Use Euclidean distance and start with A1, B1, and C1 as the initial cluster centers.

Step 1: Initialization We initialize the cluster centers:

- Cluster 1: $A1(2, 10)$
- Cluster 2: $B1(5, 8)$
- Cluster 3: $C1(1, 2)$

Step 2: Assignment We calculate the distance from each point to each cluster center using the Euclidean distance formula:

$$\text{Distance} = \sqrt{(x_2 - x_1)^2 + (y_2 - y_1)^2}$$

Point	A1	B1	C1	Assigned Cluster
$A1$	0	3.61	8.06	Cluster 1
$A2$	5	3.16	9.22	Cluster 2
$A3$	8.24	6.08	7.21	Cluster 1
$B1$	3.61	0	7.07	Cluster 1
$B2$	5.39	3.61	8.06	Cluster 2
$B3$	5	2.24	7.07	Cluster 2
$C1$	8.06	7.07	0	Cluster 3
$C2$	8.06	5	8.06	Cluster 2

Step 3: Update We calculate the mean of the points in each cluster to update the cluster centers:

- Cluster 1 mean: $\left(\frac{2+2+8}{3}, \frac{10+5+4}{3}\right) = (4, 6.33)$
- Cluster 2 mean: $\left(\frac{5+7+6}{3}, \frac{8+5+4}{3}\right) = (6, 5.67)$
- Cluster 3 mean: $\left(\frac{1+4}{2}, \frac{2+9}{2}\right) = (2.5, 5.5)$

Step 4: Repeat After the first round, we have already converged.
(a) The three cluster centers after the first round of execution:

- Cluster 1 center: $(4, 6.33)$
- Cluster 2 center: $(6, 5.67)$
- Cluster 3 center: $(2.5, 5.5)$

(b) The final three clusters:

- Cluster 1: $A1, A2, A3$
- Cluster 2: $B1, B2, B3$
- Cluster 3: $C1, C2$

5.6.4 K-Means implementation in R

In the above example, we first load the iris dataset. We then use the `kmeans()` function to fit the K-Means model to the first four columns of the iris dataset, which represent the predictor variables. The `centers` argument is set to k, which is the number of clusters we want to form.

We then print the cluster centers using `kmeans_model$centers`.

Finally, we plot the clusters using ggplot2 and `factor(kmeans_model$cluster)` to color the points according to their assigned cluster.

Note that the optimal number of clusters is often not known in advance and may require some experimentation. You can use various metrics such as the within-cluster sum of squares (WSS) or silhouette score to evaluate the quality of the clustering results for different values of K.

5.7 Advanced Data Analysis and Integration with R

Time Series Data Time series data is collected over a period of time, with measurements taken at regular intervals. It can be viewed as a sequence of data points representing specific times and corresponding values. Examples of time series data include stock prices, weather measurements, sales data, website traffic, and sensor data.

Table 5.3: Classification of Iris Species using K-Means clustering in R

```
# Load the iris dataset
data(iris)

# Fit the K-Means model
set.seed(123)
k <- 3 # number of clusters
kmeans_model <- kmeans(iris[, 1:4], centers = k)

# Print the cluster centers
print(kmeans_model$centers)

# Plot the clusters
library(ggplot2)
ggplot(iris, aes(x = Sepal.Length,
                 y = Sepal.Width,
                 color = factor(kmeans_model$cluster))) +
                 geom_point() +labs(color = "Cluster")
```

Time series data is often analyzed using techniques such as forecasting, trend analysis, and seasonality analysis. These methods help identify patterns and trends and make predictions about future values based on past behavior.

5.7.1 Time Series Analysis

Time series analysis is a statistical technique used to model and analyze time series data. It involves identifying patterns, trends, and relationships within the data to understand and predict future behavior.

In R, time series analysis can be performed using various built-in packages. The process typically involves:

- Loading the data from CSV files, Excel files, or databases using functions like `read.csv()`, `read_excel()`, or `dbGetQuery()`.
- Transforming the data into time series objects using functions like `ts()`, `xts()`, or `zoo()`.
- Visualizing the data using packages like ggplot2, `lattice`, or `tsplot`.
- Modeling the time series using packages like `forecast`, `stats`, or `ARIMA`.
- Evaluating model performance using metrics like Mean Absolute Error (MAE), Mean Squared Error (MSE), and Root Mean Squared Error (RMSE).
- Forecasting future values using the `forecast()` function.

Example of Time Series Analysis in R

```
# Load the data
data <- read.csv("sales.csv", header = TRUE, sep = ",")

# Transform the data into a time series object
ts_data <- ts(data$Sales, start = c(2017, 1),
                     end = c(2021, 12), frequency = 12)

# Visualize the data
library(ggplot2)
ggplot(data, aes(x = Month, y = Sales)) +
  geom_line() +
  xlab("Month") +
  ylab("Sales") +
  ggtitle("Sales over time")

# Fit a seasonal ARIMA model
library(forecast)
```

```
fit <- auto.arima(ts_data)

# Evaluate the model
accuracy(fit)

# Forecast future sales
forecast_data <- forecast(fit, h = 12)
plot(forecast_data, main = "Forecasted Sales")
```

In this example, we load sales data from a CSV file and transform it into a time series object. We visualize the data using `ggplot2`, fit a seasonal ARIMA model using `auto.arima()`, evaluate the model's accuracy, and forecast future sales using `forecast()`.

5.8 Social Network Analysis in Data Science

Social network analysis is a powerful tool in data science for analyzing and visualizing complex networks and understanding the relationships and connections between individuals or groups. It can be used in various applications, including:

1. **Identify key players:** Social network analysis helps identify influential individuals or groups within a network who may have a significant impact on its behavior or dynamics.

2. **Predict behavior:** By analyzing patterns of interactions and communication, social network analysis can predict future behavior, such as the likelihood of adopting a new behavior or idea.

3. **Study the spread of information:** It can be used to study the diffusion of information or ideas within a network and identify factors contributing to its spread.

4. **Detect communities:** Social network analysis identifies subgroups or communities within the network, each with different characteristics or behavior patterns.

5. **Visualize networks:** Creating visualizations of complex networks helps identify patterns and structures within the network.

Social network analysis finds applications in social media analysis, marketing research, epidemiology, and organizational analysis. With the growth of social media and online platforms, it has become increasingly important in data science for understanding and analyzing the dynamics of complex networks.

5.9 Reading data from Relational databases

Reading Data from MySQL Database in R using RMySQL

In R, you can read data from a MySQL database using the RMySQL package. Here are the steps to follow:

1. **Install the RMySQL package:** Use the following command to install the RMySQL package:

   ```
   install.packages("RMySQL")
   ```

2. **Load the package:** Use the following command to load the RMySQL package:

   ```
   library(RMySQL)
   ```

3. **Connect to the database:** Use the `dbConnect` function to connect to the MySQL database. The function takes the following arguments:

   - `drv`: The name of the database driver to use (in this case, "MySQL").
   - `dbname`: The name of the database to connect to.
   - `host`: The host name or IP address of the server.
   - `port`: The port number to use for the connection.
   - `user`: The username to use for the connection.
   - `password`: The password to use for the connection.

   ```
   con <- dbConnect(MySQL(), dbname = "database_name",
                    host = "localhost",
                    port = 3306,
                    user = "username",
                    password = "password")
   ```

4. **Query the database:** Use the `dbGetQuery` function to execute a SQL query on the database and retrieve the results as a data frame.

   ```
   result <- dbGetQuery(con, "SELECT * FROM table_name")
   ```

5. **Close the connection:** Use the `dbDisconnect` function to close the connection to the database.

   dbDisconnect(con)

Note that you may need to install the MySQL database and configure it before you can connect to it using RMySQL. Also, make sure that you have the necessary privileges to access the database and tables you are trying to query.

Here is an example code snippet that shows how to connect to a MySQL database and read data from a table:

Table 5.4: R Code for Connecting to a MySQL Database

```
# Load the RMySQL package
library(RMySQL)

# Establish a connection to the database
con <- dbConnect(MySQL(),
          user="yourusername",
          password="yourpassword",
          dbname="yourdatabase",
          host="yourhost")

# Read data from a table
data <- dbGetQuery(con, "SELECT * FROM yourtable")

# Close the connection
dbDisconnect(con)
```

5.10 Reading Data from MongoDB

To read data from a MongoDB database in R, you can use the `mongolite` package. Here's an example code snippet that demonstrates how to connect to a MongoDB database and read data from a collection:

```
# Load the mongolite package
library(mongolite)

# Connect to the MongoDB database
con <- mongo(collection = "your_collection", db = "your_database")

# Read data from the collection
data <- con$find()

# Close the connection
con$disconnect()
```

In this code, you first load the `mongolite` package, which provides functions for connecting to and working with MongoDB databases. You then establish a connection to the MongoDB database using the `mongo()` function, which takes arguments for the name of the collection and the name of the database.

Once you have established a connection, you can use the `$find()` method to read data from the collection. This method returns a data frame containing the results of the query.

Finally, you use the `$disconnect()` method to close the connection to the MongoDB database.

5.11 Exercises

5.11.1 Short and Long Answer Questions

1. Describe the key performance measures used in classification algorithms and explain their significance in evaluating model performance.

2. Walk through the implementation of logistic regression in R, including how to prepare data, train the model, and evaluate its performance.

3. Discuss the K-Nearest Neighbors (KNN) algorithm and its implementation in R. Provide insights into how the algorithm works and its practical applications.

4. Compare and contrast the implementation of K-Means clustering algorithm with other clustering algorithms in R. Discuss the advantages and limitations of K-Means.

5. Explain the steps involved in conducting time series analysis using R. Discuss common techniques and packages used for analyzing time series data.

6. Describe the process of performing social network analysis in R. Discuss the key metrics and visualizations used to analyze social network data.

7. Explain how to read data from relational databases like MySQL into R.

8. Discuss the R packages and methods used for connecting to and querying relational databases.

9. Describe the process of reading data from NoSQL databases like MongoDB into R. Discuss the R packages and methods used for connecting to and querying NoSQL databases.

10. Discuss the challenges and considerations involved in working with large datasets in R. Provide strategies and techniques for efficient data handling and processing.

11. Explain the concept of data preprocessing in the context of machine learning and data analysis. Discuss common preprocessing techniques and their implementation in R.

12. Consider a dataset with the following points in a two-dimensional space:

$$\{(2,3),(4,6),(5,4),(7,5),(8,7),(9,4),(6,2),(3,7)\}$$

Apply the K-Means clustering algorithm with $k = 3$ clusters. Show the initialization of centroids, the assignment of points to clusters, and the update of centroids for each iteration until convergence.

13. Consider a dataset with the following points in a two-dimensional space:

$$\{(1,2),(2,1),(2,3),(3,2),(4,3),(5,4),(6,5),(7,6),(8,7),(9,8)\}$$

Suppose we want to classify a new point $(4.5, 5)$ using the KNN algorithm with $k = 3$. Determine the three nearest neighbors of the new point based on Euclidean distance and classify the point using the majority class among its neighbors.

5.11.2 Fill in the Blanks

1. In logistic regression, the output is the probability of a particular outcome being ______.

2. K-Nearest Neighbors (KNN) algorithm is a type of ______ learning.

3. In K-Means clustering, the objective is to minimize the ______ within clusters.

4. Time series analysis involves analyzing data points collected ______.

5. Social network analysis focuses on studying the relationships and interactions among ______.

6. Reading data from relational databases like MySQL in R can be done using the ______ package.

7. MongoDB is an example of a ______ database.

8. A confusion matrix is used to evaluate the performance of a classification model by comparing predicted and ______ values.

9. The silhouette score is a metric used to evaluate the performance of ______ algorithms.

10. In time series analysis, the Autoregressive Integrated Moving Average (ARIMA) model is used to forecast future ______ based on historical data.

5.11.3 Multiple Choice Questions

1. What is a common performance measure used in classification?
   A) Mean Absolute Error
   B) Root Mean Squared Error
   C) Accuracy
   D) Variance

2. In logistic regression, what type of function is used to model the relationship between variables?
   A) Sigmoid function
   B) Linear function
   C) Exponential function
   D) Logarithmic function

3. What does K-Nearest Neighbors (KNN) algorithm do in classification?
   A) Fits a linear regression line
   B) Calculates the distance between data points
   C) Finds the optimal decision boundary
   D) Divides the dataset into clusters

4. Which statement about the K-Nearest Neighbors (KNN) algorithm is correct?
   A) KNN is a parametric model
   B) KNN works well with high-dimensional data
   C) KNN is not affected by outliers
   D) KNN does not require a training phase

5. What is the objective of the K-Means clustering algorithm?
   A) To classify data into distinct categories
   B) To find the nearest neighbors for each data point
   C) To minimize the variance within clusters
   D) To maximize the variance between clusters

6. Which of the following is a step in the K-Means algorithm?
   A) Randomly assign data points to clusters
   B) Compute the Euclidean distance between data points
   C) Merge clusters with the least variance
   D) Update cluster centroids based on the mean of data points

7. What is the purpose of time series analysis in R?
   A) To predict future events based on historical data
   B) To analyze spatial data
   C) To perform sentiment analysis
   D) To visualize network graphs

8. What is a common technique used in social network analysis?
   A) Hierarchical clustering
   B) PageRank algorithm
   C) K-Means clustering
   D) Linear regression

9. How do you read data from a MySQL database in R?
   A) Using read.csv() function
   B) Using read.table() function
   C) Using readSQL() function
   D) Using read.db() function

10. Which database is commonly used for NoSQL data storage?
    A) PostgreSQL
    B) SQLite
    C) MongoDB
    D) MariaDB

11. What does the term "performance measures" typically refer to in classification?
    A) Metrics used to evaluate the speed of algorithms
    B) Metrics used to evaluate the accuracy of classification models
    C) Metrics used to evaluate the complexity of classification models
    D) Metrics used to evaluate the scalability of classification models

12. In logistic regression implementation in R, what function is commonly used to fit the model?
    A) lm()
    B) glm()
    C) knn()
    D) kmeans()

13. What does the K-Nearest Neighbors (KNN) algorithm use to make predictions?
    A) Probability density functions
    B) Conditional probability
    C) Majority vote of nearest neighbors
    D) Mean of nearest neighbors

14. In K-Means implementation in R, what function is commonly used to perform clustering?
    A) kmeans()
    B) knn()
    C) kmeans.cluster()
    D) kmeans.fit()

15. What is a characteristic of time series data?
    A) It has no temporal component
    B) Observations are independent of each other
    C) Observations are recorded at regular intervals
    D) Observations are not ordered chronologically

16. What is an example of a social network analysis metric?
    A) Mean squared error
    B) Betweenness centrality
    C) Correlation coefficient
    D) Variance

17. How do you connect R to a MongoDB database?
    A) Using read.csv() function
    B) Using read.table() function
    C) Using readMongo() function
    D) Using read.db() function

18. What is a common application of logistic regression in classification tasks?
    A) Image recognition
    B) Sentiment analysis
    C) Clustering
    D) Network analysis

19. What is the main goal of the K-Means algorithm?
    A) To find the optimal decision boundary
    B) To divide data points into distinct clusters
    C) To calculate the distance between data points
    D) To perform dimensionality reduction

Chapter 6

Association Rule Mining

6.1 Introduction

Association rule mining is a fundamental technique in data mining and machine learning used to discover interesting relationships between variables in large datasets. It is particularly useful for uncovering hidden patterns, correlations, or dependencies among items or variables.

At its core, association rule mining aims to find associations, or rules, between different items in a dataset. These rules are often in the form of "if-then" statements, indicating that if certain items occur together, then other items are likely to occur as well.

For example, in a retail transaction dataset, association rule mining might reveal that customers who purchase bread are also likely to purchase butter. This insight can be valuable for marketing strategies, such as placing butter near the bread aisle to increase sales.

The process of association rule mining typically involves two main steps:

1. **Frequent Itemset Generation**: This step involves identifying sets of items that frequently occur together in the dataset. These sets are called frequent itemsets. By determining which combinations of items are frequent, we can focus our analysis on the most relevant patterns.

2. **Rule Generation**: Once frequent itemsets are identified, association rules are generated from them. These rules express relationships between items, with metrics like support, confidence, and lift used to evaluate the significance and reliability of the rules.

Example

Consider a dataset containing transactions at a grocery store. Let's say we have the following transaction table 6.1.

Let's find the frequent itemsets with a minimum support of 60

Table 6.1: Transactions

TID	Items
1	Bread, Milk
2	Bread, Diapers, Beer, Eggs
3	Milk, Diapers, Beer, Coke
4	Bread, Milk, Diapers, Beer
5	Bread, Milk, Diapers, Coke

Table 6.2: Frequent Itemsets

Frequent Itemset	Support
{Bread, Milk}	4/5 (80%)
{Diapers, Beer}	3/5 (60%)
{Bread, Diapers}	3/5 (60%)
{Milk, Diapers}	3/5 (60%)

Let's consider the frequent itemset Bread, Milk and find an association rule with a minimum confidence of 70

- Association Rule: Bread $\rightarrow$ Milk with confidence = (support(Bread, Milk) / support(Bread)) = (4/5) / (4/5) = 100

This indicates that whenever Bread is purchased, Milk is also purchased with a confidence of 100

Association rule mining finds applications in diverse domains. It enables Market Basket Analysis, facilitating an understanding of customer purchasing behavior in retail stores. Moreover, it aids in Cross-selling and Upselling efforts by recommending additional products or services to customers based on their current selections. In Web Usage Mining, association rule mining assists in analyzing website navigation patterns, thereby enhancing user experience and content delivery. Healthcare benefits from association rule mining by identifying associations between medical conditions and patient demographics for disease diagnosis and treatment. Additionally, it plays a crucial role in Fraud Detection, where it helps in discovering unusual patterns or behaviors in financial transactions, aiding in the detection of fraudulent activities.

6.2 Algorithms for Association Rule Mining

1. **Apriori Algorithm**: One of the most popular algorithms for mining frequent itemsets and generating association rules. It uses a bottom-up approach where frequent itemsets are iteratively generated and used to explore larger itemsets.

2. **FP-Growth (Frequent Pattern Growth)**: An alternative approach to Apriori, which represents the dataset in a compact data structure called a FP-tree and uses pattern fragment growth to mine frequent itemsets.

3. **Eclat Algorithm**: Similar to Apriori but uses a depth-first search strategy to mine frequent itemsets.

4. **CARMA (Classification based on Association Rule Mining)**: Utilizes association rule mining to generate classification rules.

The **Apriori** algorithm begins by identifying frequent individual items in the dataset. It then generates candidate itemsets of size k by joining frequent $(k-1)$-itemsets. These candidate itemsets are pruned to eliminate those containing infrequent subsets. The support for each remaining candidate itemset is calculated to determine its frequency of occurrence in the dataset. Next, candidate itemsets of size $k+1$ are generated from the frequent k-itemsets, and the process of pruning and support calculation is repeated. This cycle continues iteratively until no more frequent itemsets can be generated, at which point the algorithm terminates.

6.3 Measures of Finding Interesting Patterns

Association rule mining involves uncovering valuable insights from data by identifying patterns, relationships, and dependencies among items or variables. A crucial aspect of association rule mining is the evaluation of these discovered patterns, which is accomplished through measures designed to quantify their significance and reliability.

The measures of finding interesting patterns in association rule mining serve as essential tools for assessing the strength and relevance of discovered rules. These measures provide valuable insights into the frequency, reliability, and potential significance of association rules in the dataset.

The measures of association rule mining encompass several key metrics that evaluate the significance and reliability of discovered patterns. Support quantifies the frequency of occurrence of an itemset, indicating its prevalence among transactions. Confidence assesses the reliability of association rules by measuring the conditional probability of finding the consequent item given the antecedent. Lift evaluates the strength of association between antecedent and consequent items, highlighting deviations from statistical independence. Leverage measures the difference between observed and expected itemset frequency, offering insights into association significance. Conviction assesses the strength of a rule by comparing the frequency of antecedent occurrence with and without the consequent. Together, these metrics provide comprehensive insights into the characteristics and strength of association rules mined from data.

Table 6.3: Measures of Finding Interesting Patterns

Measure	Formula
Support	$\frac{\text{Frequency of itemset}}{\text{Total transactions}}$
Confidence	$\frac{\text{Support}(A \cup B)}{\text{Support}(A)}$
Lift	$\frac{\text{Support}(A \cup B)}{\text{Support}(A) \times \text{Support}(B)}$
Leverage	$\text{Support}(A \cup B) - (\text{Support}(A) \times \text{Support}(B))$
Conviction	$\frac{\text{Support}(A) \times (1 - \text{Support}(B))}{\text{Support}(A \setminus B)}$

6.4 R Code for Finding frequent itemset and Generating Rules

Table 6.4: Compute frequent itemsets and generate association rules

```
# Install and load the arules package
install.packages("arules")
library(arules)

# Create a transaction dataset
transactions <- list(
  c("Bread", "Milk"),
  c("Bread", "Diapers","Beer","Eggs"),
  c("Milk", "Diapers", "Beer","Coke"),
  c("Bread", "Milk","Diapers","Beer"),
  c("Bread", "Milk", "Diapers", "Coke")
)

# Convert transactions to transactions class
trans <- as(transactions, "transactions")

# Find frequent itemsets using the Apriori algorithm
itemsets <- apriori(trans, parameter = list(support = 0.4, minlen = 2))

# Generate association rules
rules <- apriori(trans, parameter = list(support = 0.4, confidence = 0.7))

# Display frequent itemsets
inspect(itemsets)

# Display association rules
inspect(rules)
```

6.5 Finding Frequent Itemsets using Apriori

The Apriori algorithm starts by scanning the dataset to identify individual items (1-itemsets) and count their occurrences, retaining those that meet a minimum support threshold. Using these frequent 1-itemsets, it generates candidate 2-itemsets, which are then pruned based on the same support threshold. This process is repeated iteratively for higher-order itemsets (3-itemsets, 4-itemsets, etc.) until no more frequent itemsets can be identified. Afterward, the algorithm generates association rules from the frequent itemsets by evaluating the confidence of each rule, retaining those that meet a predefined minimum confidence threshold.

Table 6.5: Apriori Algorithm Example

Step	Description
1	Find frequent 1-itemsets Bread: 4 Milk: 4 Diapers: 4 Beer: 3 Coke: 2 Eggs: 1
2	Generate candidate 2-itemsets {Bread, Milk} {Bread, Diapers} {Milk, Diapers}
3	Prune candidate 2-itemsets {Bread, Milk} {Bread, Diapers} {Milk, Diapers}
4	Find support for candidate 2-itemsets {Bread, Milk}: 3 {Bread, Diapers}: 3 {Milk, Diapers}: 3
5	Generate candidate 3-itemsets {Bread, Milk, Diapers}
6	Prune candidate 3-itemsets {Bread, Milk, Diapers}
7	Find support for candidate 3-itemsets {Bread, Milk, Diapers}: 3
8	Stop Since there are no candidate k-itemsets generated, the algorithm stops.

6.6 Rules Generation

Table 6.6: Association Rules

Association Rule	Support	Confidence
{Bread, Milk} → {Diapers}	4/5 (80%)	4/4 (100%)
{Bread, Diapers} → {Milk}	3/5 (60%)	3/4 (75%)
{Milk, Diapers} → {Bread}	3/5 (60%)	3/4 (75%)

6.7 Exercises

6.7.1 Short and Long Answer Questions

1. What is association rule mining?
2. What is the Apriori principle in association rule mining?
3. What is the difference between frequent itemsets and association rules?
4. How does the Lift measure help in evaluating association rules?
5. What are pattern interestingness measures in association rule mining?
6. Explain the Apriori algorithm step by step and how it works to mine frequent itemsets.
7. Discuss the significance of support and confidence measures in association rule mining. Provide examples to illustrate their importance.
8. Describe the challenges and limitations of association rule mining, and discuss strategies to address these challenges.
9. Discuss pattern interestingness measures in association rule mining, including support, confidence, lift, leverage, and conviction. Explain how each measure contributes to evaluating the significance and reliability of discovered rules.
10. Provide a detailed explanation of at least three real-world applications of association rule mining, highlighting the benefits and challenges in each application domain.

6.7.2 Fill in the Blanks

1. The Apriori algorithm is commonly used for mining frequent ___________.
2. Lift measures the strength of association between antecedent and consequent compared to ___________.

3. Conviction assesses the ratio of the expected frequency that the antecedent occurs without the consequent to the frequency that the antecedent occurs without regard to the ___________.

4. The support measure in association rule mining quantifies the frequency of occurrence of an itemset in the ___________.

5. Pattern interestingness measures provide insights into the significance and ___________ of discovered rules.

6.7.3 Multiple choice Questions

1. What is association rule mining?
   (a) A technique for finding patterns in data
   (b) A method for classifying data into categories
   (c) A statistical approach for regression analysis
   (d) A strategy for clustering similar data points

2. What is the Apriori principle in association rule mining?
   (a) It is a principle that states that all frequent itemsets must be stored in memory.
   (b) It is a principle that states that a subset of a frequent itemset must also be frequent.
   (c) It is a principle that states that only the maximal frequent itemsets are considered in mining.
   (d) It is a principle that states that the minimum support threshold should be set to zero.

3. What is the difference between frequent itemsets and association rules?
   (a) Frequent itemsets contain only one item, while association rules contain multiple items.
   (b) Frequent itemsets are the input to association rule mining, while association rules are the output.
   (c) Frequent itemsets have high support, while association rules have high confidence.
   (d) Frequent itemsets are generated using the FP-Growth algorithm, while association rules are generated using the Apriori algorithm.

4. How does the Lift measure help in evaluating association rules?
   (a) It measures the frequency of occurrence of an itemset in the dataset.

   (b) It measures the reliability of the association rule by assessing the conditional probability.
   (c) It evaluates the strength of association between antecedent and consequent, compared to statistical independence.
   (d) It measures the difference between the observed frequency and the expected frequency of the itemset.

5. What are pattern interestingness measures in association rule mining?
   (a) Measures used to assess the quality of the dataset
   (b) Measures used to evaluate the performance of association rule mining algorithms
   (c) Measures used to quantify the significance and reliability of discovered rules
   (d) Measures used to determine the complexity of the association rule mining process

6. Which algorithm is commonly used for frequent itemset mining?
   (a) K-means
   (b) Decision Tree
   (c) Apriori
   (d) SVM

7. What does the support measure indicate in association rule mining?
   (a) The reliability of the association rule
   (b) The frequency of occurrence of an itemset in the dataset
   (c) The difference between observed and expected frequencies
   (d) The strength of association between antecedent and consequent

8. Which of the following is a limitation of the Apriori algorithm?
   (a) It cannot handle large datasets
   (b) It requires multiple passes over the dataset
   (c) It cannot find all frequent itemsets efficiently
   (d) It is not suitable for binary data

9. What is leverage in association rule mining?
   (a) The ratio of observed to expected frequency of an itemset
   (b) The difference between observed and expected frequencies of an itemset
   (c) The ratio of support for antecedent to support for consequent
   (d) The conditional probability of finding consequent given antecedent

10. Which measure helps in assessing the reliability of an association rule?
    (a) Support
    (b) Confidence
    (c) Lift
    (d) Leverage

Chapter 7

Additional Experiments

1. **To get the input from user and perform numerical operations (MAX, MIN, AVG, SUM, SQRT, ROUND) in R**

```r
# Prompt user to enter numbers
input<-readline(prompt ="Enter numbers separated by spaces:")
# Split the input string into a numeric vector
numbers <- as.numeric(unlist(strsplit(input, " ")))

# Maximum value
max_value <- max(numbers)
print(paste("Maximum: ", max_value))
# Minimum value
min_value <- min(numbers)
print(paste("Minimum: ", min_value))
# Average value
avg_value <- mean(numbers)
print(paste("Average: ", avg_value))
# Sum
sum_value <- sum(numbers)
print(paste("Sum: ", sum_value))
# Square Roots
sqrt_values <- sqrt(numbers)
print("Square roots: ")
print(sqrt_values)
# Round to 2 decimal places
rounded_values <- round(numbers, 2)
print("Rounded values: ")
print(rounded_values)
```

2. To perform data import/export (CSV, XLS, TXT) operations using data frames in R.

CSV Files

Using base R:

```
# Importing CSV using base R
data <- read.csv("path/to/your/file.csv")
```

Using `readr`:

```
# Install readr package if not already installed
install.packages("readr")

# Importing CSV using readr
library(readr)
data <- read_csv("path/to/your/file.csv")
```

XLS/XLSX Files

Using `readxl`:

```
# Install readxl package if not already installed
install.packages("readxl")

# Importing Excel files
library(readxl)
data <- read_excel("path/to/your/file.xlsx", sheet = "Sheet1")
```

TXT Files

Using base R:

```
# Importing TXT using base R
data <- read.table("path/to/your/file.txt",
                   header = TRUE, sep = "\t")
```

Using `readr`:

```
# Importing TXT using readr
library(readr)
data <- read_tsv("path/to/your/file.txt")
```

Exporting Data

CSV Files

Using base R:

```
# Exporting CSV using base R
write.csv(data, "path/to/save/your/file.csv", row.names = FALSE)
```

Using **readr**:

```
# Exporting CSV using readr
library(readr)
write_csv(data, "path/to/save/your/file.csv")
```

XLS/XLSX Files

Using **writexl**:

```
# Install writexl package if not already installed
install.packages("writexl")

# Exporting Excel files
library(writexl)
write_xlsx(data, "path/to/save/your/file.xlsx")
```

TXT Files

Using base R:

```
# Exporting TXT using base R
write.table(data,
"path/to/save/your/file.txt", sep = "\t",
 row.names = FALSE)
```

Using **readr**:

```
# Exporting TXT using readr
library(readr)
write_tsv(data, "path/to/save/your/file.txt")
```

3. To get the input matrix from user and perform Matrix addition, subtraction, multiplication,inverse transpose AND division operations using vector concept in R.

Matrix Operations in R

Getting Input Matrix from User

```
# Define the size of the matrix
n <- as.integer(readline(prompt="Enter the number of rows: "))
m <- as.integer(readline(prompt="Enter the number of columns: "))

# Read matrix elements from user
cat("Enter the elements of the first matrix (row-wise):\n")
matrix_elements_1 <- as.numeric(unlist(strsplit(readline(), " ")))
matrix_1 <- matrix(matrix_elements_1, nrow = n, ncol = m, byrow = TRUE)

cat("Enter the elements of the second matrix (row-wise):\n")
matrix_elements_2 <- as.numeric(unlist(strsplit(readline(), " ")))
matrix_2 <- matrix(matrix_elements_2, nrow = n, ncol = m, byrow = TRUE)

# Display the matrices
cat("First Matrix:\n")
print(matrix_1)
cat("Second Matrix:\n")
print(matrix_2)
```

Matrix Addition

```
# Matrix Addition
matrix_add <- matrix_1 + matrix_2
cat("Matrix Addition:\n")
print(matrix_add)
```

Matrix Subtraction

```
# Matrix Subtraction
matrix_sub <- matrix_1 - matrix_2
cat("Matrix Subtraction:\n")
print(matrix_sub)
```

Matrix Multiplication

```
# Matrix Multiplication
matrix_mul <- matrix_1 %*% matrix_2
cat("Matrix Multiplication:\n")
print(matrix_mul)
```

Matrix Inverse

```
# Matrix Inverse
matrix_inv <- solve(matrix_1)
cat("Matrix Inverse:\n")
print(matrix_inv)
```

Matrix Transpose

```
# Matrix Transpose
matrix_transpose <- t(matrix_1)
cat("Matrix Transpose:\n")
print(matrix_transpose)
```

Matrix Division

```
# Matrix Division

matrix_div <- matrix_1 / matrix_2
cat("Matrix Division:\n")
print(matrix_div)
```

4. To perform statistical operations (Mean, Median, Mode and Standard deviation) using R.

Statistical Operations in R

```
# Function to calculate mode
calculate_mode <- function(x) {
  uniqx <- unique(x)
  uniqx[which.max(tabulate(match(x, uniqx)))]
}

# Read numeric vector from user
cat("Enter the elements of the numeric vector separated by spaces:\n")
vector_elements <- as.numeric(unlist(strsplit(readline(), " ")))

# Calculate Mean
mean_value <- mean(vector_elements)
cat("Mean:\n")
print(mean_value)

# Calculate Median
median_value <- median(vector_elements)
cat("Median:\n")
print(median_value)

# Calculate Mode
mode_value <- calculate_mode(vector_elements)
cat("Mode:\n")
print(mode_value)

# Calculate Standard Deviation
sd_value <- sd(vector_elements)
cat("Standard Deviation:\n")
print(sd_value)
```

5. **To perform data pre-processing operations**

i) Handling Missing data
ii) Min-Max normalization.

Data Pre-processing Operations in R

Handling Missing Data

```
# Create a sample data frame with missing values
data <- data.frame(
  ID = 1:5,
  Age = c(25, NA, 30, NA, 45),
  Score = c(80, 90, NA, 70, 85)
)
# Display the original data
cat("Original Data:\n")
print(data)
# Option 1: Remove rows with missing values
data_no_na <- na.omit(data)
cat("Data after removing rows with missing values:\n")
print(data_no_na)
# Option 2: Replace missing values with the mean (for numeric columns)
data_imputed <- data
data_imputed$Age[is.na(data_imputed$Age)]
<- mean(data_imputed$Age, na.rm = TRUE)
data_imputed$Score[is.na(data_imputed$Score)]
<- mean(data_imputed$Score, na.rm = TRUE)
cat("Data after replacing missing values with the mean:\n")
print(data_imputed)
```

Min-Max Normalization

```
# Function to perform Min-Max normalization
min_max_normalize <- function(x) {
  return((x - min(x, na.rm = TRUE)) /
                (max(x, na.rm = TRUE) - min(x, na.rm = TRUE)))
}
# Apply Min-Max normalization to the numeric columns
data_normalized <- data
data_normalized$Age <- min_max_normalize(data$Age)
data_normalized$Score <- min_max_normalize(data$Score)
# Display the normalized data
cat("Data after Min-Max normalization:\n")
print(data_normalized)
```

6. To perform dimensionality reduction operation using PCA for Houses Data Set.

```
# Load necessary libraries
install.packages("ggplot2")  # For visualization (optional)
install.packages("caret")    # For data splitting (optional)
library(ggplot2)
library(caret)

# Load your dataset
# Example: data <- read.csv("path/to/your/houses_data.csv")
data <- data.frame(
  Price = c(300000, 450000, 500000, 600000, 700000),
  SqFt = c(1500, 2000, 1800, 2200, 2500),
  Bedrooms = c(3, 4, 3, 5, 4),
  Bathrooms = c(2, 3, 2, 3, 4)
)

# View the first few rows of the dataset
cat("Original Data:\n")
print(head(data))

# Remove non-numeric columns if any
data_numeric <- data[, sapply(data, is.numeric)]

# Standardize the data (important for PCA)
data_scaled <- scale(data_numeric)

# Perform PCA
pca_result <- prcomp(data_scaled, center = TRUE, scale. = TRUE)

# Summary of PCA results
cat("PCA Summary:\n")
print(summary(pca_result))

# Print principal components
cat("Principal Components:\n")
print(pca_result$rotation)

# Print the scores of the principal components
cat("PCA Scores:\n")
print(pca_result$x)
# Plotting the PCA results (optional)
# Scree plot to visualize variance explained by each principal component
screeplot(pca_result, main="Scree Plot")
# Biplot to visualize the principal components
biplot(pca_result, main="PCA Biplot")
```

7. To perform Simple Linear Regression with R.

```
# Load necessary libraries (if not already installed)
# install.packages("ggplot2")
library(ggplot2)

# Create a sample data frame
data <- data.frame(
  X = c(1, 2, 3, 4, 5),
  Y = c(2, 4, 5, 4, 6)
)

# View the first few rows of the dataset
cat("Original Data:\n")
print(data)

# Fit a simple linear regression model
model <- lm(Y ~ X, data = data)

# Summary of the model
cat("Model Summary:\n")
print(summary(model))

# Predict values using the model
data$Predicted_Y <- predict(model, newdata = data)

# Display the data with predictions
cat("Data with Predicted Values:\n")
print(data)

# Plot the data and the regression line
ggplot(data, aes(x = X, y = Y)) +
  geom_point() +
  geom_smooth(method = "lm", se = FALSE, color = "blue") +
  labs(title = "Simple Linear Regression", x = "X", y = "Y") +
  theme_minimal()
```

8. To perform K-Means clustering operation and visualize for iris data set.

```
# Install ggplot2 if not already installed
if (!require(ggplot2)) {
  install.packages("ggplot2")
}

# Load necessary libraries
library(ggplot2)  # For visualization
library(datasets) # For the Iris dataset

# Load the Iris dataset
data(iris)

# Prepare the data for clustering
iris_data <- iris[, 1:4]  # Select only the feature columns

# Perform K-Means clustering with 3 clusters
set.seed(123)  # Set seed for reproducibility
kmeans_result <- kmeans(iris_data, centers = 3, nstart = 20)

# Add the cluster assignments to the original data
iris$Cluster <- as.factor(kmeans_result$cluster)

# Plot Sepal.Length vs Sepal.Width colored by cluster
ggplot(iris, aes(x = Sepal.Length, y = Sepal.Width,
color = Cluster)) +
  geom_point(size = 3) +
  labs(title = "K-Means Clustering of Iris Dataset",
       x = "Sepal Length",
       y = "Sepal Width") +
  theme_minimal()

# Plot Petal.Length vs Petal.Width colored by cluster
ggplot(iris, aes(x = Petal.Length, y = Petal.Width,
color = Cluster)) +
  geom_point(size = 3) +
  labs(title = "K-Means Clustering of Iris Dataset",
       x = "Petal Length",
       y = "Petal Width") +
  theme_minimal()
```

9. Learn how to collect data via web-scraping. APIs and data connectors from suitable sources as specified the instructor.

Web Scraping

```
# Install required packages
install.packages("rvest")
# Load the library
library(rvest)
 Define the URL of the website
url <- 'https://posit.co/resources/cheatsheets/'
 Read the HTML content from the website
webpage <- read_html(url)
# Extract and print the title of the webpage
title <- webpage %>% html_node("title") %>% html_text()
print(paste("Title of the webpage:", title))
# Extract and print all hyperlinks on the page
links <- webpage %>% html_nodes("a") %>% html_attr("href")
print("Links on the webpage:")
print(links)
```

Using APIs

```
# Install required packages
install.packages("httr")
# Load the library
library(httr)
# Define the API endpoint (Example URL)
api_url <- 'https://api.example.com/data'
# Send a GET request to the API
response <- GET(api_url)
if (status_code(response) == 200) {
  # Parse JSON response
  data <- content(response, "parsed")
  print("Data from API:")
  print(data)
} else { print("Failed to retrieve data")
}
# API Authentication Example
api_key <- 'YOUR_API_KEY'
response_auth <- GET(api_url,
add_headers(Authorization = paste("Bearer", api_key)))
if (status_code(response_auth) == 200) {
  data_auth <- content(response_auth, "parsed")
  print("Data from API with authentication:")
  print(data_auth)
} else {  print("Failed to retrieve data with authentication")}
```

Data Connectors

```
# Install and load necessary packages
install.packages("RSQLite")
install.packages("DBI")
library(DBI)
library(RSQLite)
# Connect to an SQLite database
con <- dbConnect(RSQLite::SQLite(), "example.db")
# Query the database
query <- "SELECT * FROM table_name"
df <- dbGetQuery(con, query)
# Print the DataFrame
print(df)
# Close the connection
dbDisconnect(con)
```

Using ‘dplyr‘ with SQL Databases

```
# Install and load necessary packages
install.packages("dplyr")
install.packages("dbplyr")
library(dplyr)
library(dbplyr)
# Connect to the database
con <- dbConnect(RSQLite::SQLite(), "example.db")
# Read data into a tibble using dplyr
df_dplyr <- tbl(con, "table_name") %>% collect()
# Print the DataFrame
print(df_dplyr)
# Close the connection
dbDisconnect(con)
```

Excel Spreadsheets

```
# Install and load necessary package
install.packages("readxl")
library(readxl)
# Read data from an Excel file
df_excel <- read_excel("example.xlsx")
# Print the DataFrame
print(df_excel)
```

10. Perform association analysis on a given dataset and evaluate its accuracy.

Install and Load Required Packages

```
# Install the necessary package
install.packages("arules")
# Load the library
library(arules)
```

Load and Prepare Your Dataset

```
# Load a sample dataset (e.g., Groceries dataset)
data("Groceries")
# Print a summary of the dataset
summary(Groceries)
```

Perform Association Rule Mining

```
# Perform the association rule mining
rules <- apriori(Groceries,
parameter=list(support=0.001, confidence=0.5))
# Print a summary of the rules
summary(rules)
# View the first few rules
inspect(head(rules))
```

Evaluate Association Rules

```
# Inspect the rules sorted by confidence
inspect(sort(rules, by="confidence"))
# Inspect the rules sorted by lift
inspect(sort(rules, by="lift"))
# Filter rules with high lift
high_lift_rules <- subset(rules, lift > 2)
inspect(high_lift_rules)
```

Visualize Association Rules

```
# Install and load necessary package for visualization
install.packages("arulesViz")
library(arulesViz)
# Plot rules
plot(rules, method="grouped", control=list(k=5))
```

11. Build a recommendation system on a given dataset and evaluate its accuracy.

Install and Load Required Packages

```
# Install necessary packages
install.packages(c("recommenderlab", "Matrix"))
# Load the libraries
library(recommenderlab)
library(Matrix)
```

Load and Prepare Your Dataset

```
# Example: Load a sample dataset (MovieLense)
data("MovieLense")
# Print a summary of the dataset
summary(MovieLense)
```

Create a Recommendation Model

```
# Create a recommender model using User-based collaborative filtering
rec_model <- Recommender(MovieLense, method = "UBCF")
# Print a summary of the recommender model
summary(rec_model)
```

Generate Predictions

```
# Generate predictions for all users
predictions <- predict(rec_model, MovieLense, n = 10)
# View the recommendations for the first user
as(predictions, "list")[1]
```

Evaluate the Recommendation System

```
# Split the dataset into training and test sets
train_index <- sample(1:nrow(MovieLense), size = 0.8 * nrow(MovieLense))
train_data <- MovieLense[train_index, ]
test_data <- MovieLense[-train_index, ]
# Create a recommender model on the training set
rec_model <- Recommender(train_data, method = "UBCF")
# Generate predictions on the test set
test_predictions <- predict(rec_model, test_data, n = 10)
# Evaluate the model
eval_results <- calcPredictionAccuracy(test_predictions, test_data)
print(eval_results)
```

12. Building and Evaluating a Time-Series Model Install and Load Required Packages

```
# Install necessary packages
install.packages(c("forecast", "tseries"))
# Load the libraries
library(forecast)
library(tseries)
```

Load and Preprocess the Data

```
# Load the AirPassengers dataset
data("AirPassengers")
summary(AirPassengers)
# Plot the time series
plot(AirPassengers, main="Monthly Airline Passenger Numbers 1949-1960")
```

Split the Data

```
# Define the training and test set
train_end <- length(AirPassengers) - 12  # Use last 12 months for testing
train_set <- window(AirPassengers, end=c(1959, 12))
test_set <- window(AirPassengers, start=c(1960, 1))
```

Build a Time-Series Model

```
# Fit an ARIMA model
arima_model <- auto.arima(train_set)
summary(arima_model)
# Forecast the next 12 months
forecasts <- forecast(arima_model, h=12)
# Plot the forecasts
plot(forecasts)
```

Evaluate the Model

```
# Extract forecasted values
forecast_values <- forecasts$mean
accuracy_metrics <- accuracy(forecasts, test_set)
print(accuracy_metrics)
# Plot actual vs. forecasted values
plot(test_set, main="Actual vs Forecasted Values")
lines(forecasts$mean, col="blue")
legend("topleft", legend=c("Actual", "Forecasted"), col=c("black", "blue"), lty=1:1)
```

13. Build cartographic visualization for multiple datasets involving various countries of the world;states districts and countries.

Install and Load Required Packages

```
# Install necessary packages
install.packages(c("ggplot2", "SF",
"rnaturalearth", "rnaturalearthdata",
"tmap", "dplyr"))
# Load the libraries
library(ggplot2)
library(sf)
library(rnaturalearth)
library(rnaturalearthdata)
library(tmap)
library(dplyr)
```

Load and Prepare Geospatial Data Load World Countries Data

```
# Load world countries shapefile
world <- ne_countries(scale = "medium", returnclass = "sf")
# Plot world map
ggplot(data = world) +
  geom_sf() +
  theme_minimal() +
  ggtitle("World Map")
```

Load US States Data

```
# Load US states shapefile
us_states <- ne_states(country = "United States", returnclass = "sf")
# Plot US states map
ggplot(data = us_states) +
  geom_sf() +
  theme_minimal() +
  ggtitle("US States Map")
```

Load UK Districts Data

```
# Load UK administrative boundaries (districts)
uk_districts <- ne_admin_1(country = "United Kingdom",
   returnclass = "sf")
# Plot UK districts map
ggplot(data = uk_districts) +
  geom_sf() +  theme_minimal() +  ggtitle("UK Districts Map")
```

Custom Visualizations with Data Plot Custom Data Points on a World Map

```r
# Example dataset with custom points
custom_data <- data.frame(
  name = c("Location A", "Location B"),
  lon = c(-0.1276, 2.3522),  # Example longitudes
  lat = c(51.5074, 48.8566)   # Example latitudes
)
# Convert custom data to sf object
custom_sf <- st_as_sf(custom_data, coords = c("lon", "lat"),
   crs = 4326)
# Plot custom points on world map
ggplot(data = world) +
  geom_sf() +
  geom_sf(data = custom_sf, color = "red", size = 3) +
  theme_minimal() +  ggtitle("Custom Data Points on World Map")
```

Overlay Custom Data on US States

```r
# Example dataset with data for US states
state_data <- data.frame(
  state = c("California", "New York"),
  value = c(100, 200)
)
# Merge custom data with US states data
us_states_data <- us_states %>%
  left_join(state_data, by = c("name" = "state"))
# Plot US states with custom data
ggplot(data = us_states_data) +
  geom_sf(aes(fill = value)) +
  theme_minimal() +
  ggtitle("US States with Custom Data")
```

14. Perform text mining on a set of documents and visualize the most important words in a visualization such as wand cloud.

Text Mining and Word Cloud Visualization in R
Install and Load Required Packages

```
# Install necessary packages
install.packages(c("tm", "wordcloud", "RColorBrewer", "SnowballC"))
# Load the libraries
library(tm)
library(wordcloud)
library(RColorBrewer)
library(SnowballC)
```

Load and Preprocess the Text Data

```
text_data <- readLines("path/to/your/textfile.txt")
corpus <- Corpus(VectorSource(text_data))
corpus <- tm_map(corpus, content_transformer(tolower))
corpus <- tm_map(corpus, removePunctuation)
corpus <- tm_map(corpus, removeNumbers)
corpus <- tm_map(corpus, removeWords, stopwords("en"))
corpus <- tm_map(corpus, stripWhitespace)
corpus <- tm_map(corpus, stemDocument)
```

Perform Text Mining

```
# Create a document-term matrix
dtm <- DocumentTermMatrix(corpus)
# Convert to a matrix
m <- as.matrix(dtm)
# Get word frequencies
word_freqs <- sort(rowSums(m), decreasing = TRUE)
# Create a data frame with words and their frequencies
word_freq_df <- data.frame(word = names(word_freqs), freq = word_freqs)
```

Create and Visualize the Word Cloud

```
# Create a word cloud
wordcloud(words = word_freq_df$word, freq = word_freq_df$freq,
          min.freq = 1, scale = c(3, 0.5),
          colors = brewer.pal(8, "Dark2"),
          random.order = FALSE,
          rot.per = 0.35,
          main = "Word Cloud")
```

Chapter 8

Real-world Data Science Case Studies

8.1 Insightful House Pricing

Introduction

The Boston Housing Dataset is a classic dataset in the field of machine learning and statistics. It contains information about various factors influencing housing prices in Boston suburbs, such as crime rate, number of rooms, accessibility to highways, and more. Understanding these factors and their impact on house prices is crucial for real estate analysis and investment decisions. In this case study, we will use the Boston Housing Dataset to build a predictive model that estimates the median value of owner-occupied homes (MEDV) based on other variables in the dataset.

Dataset Overview

The Boston Housing Dataset is a classic dataset often used in regression analysis and predictive modeling tasks. It contains information collected by the U.S. Census Service concerning housing in the area of Boston, Massachusetts. The dataset includes 506 instances, each representing a Boston suburb, with 14 attributes.

Objective

The objective of this case study is to develop a regression model that accurately predicts the median value of owner-occupied homes (MEDV) in Boston suburbs. By leveraging the features available in the Boston Housing Dataset, we aim to build a robust predictive model that captures the relationships between housing prices and various socio-economic factors. Through exploratory data analysis, data preprocessing, model building, evaluation, and visualization, we seek to gain insights into the factors influencing house prices and create a valuable tool for real estate valuation and decision-making.

Table 8.1: Boston Housing Dataset Attributes

Attribute	Description
CRIM	Per capita crime rate by town
ZN	Proportion of residential land zoned for lots over 25,000 sq. ft.
INDUS	Proportion of non-retail business acres per town
CHAS	Charles River dummy variable (1 if tract bounds river; 0 otherwise)
NOX	Nitric oxides concentration (parts per 10 million)
RM	Average number of rooms per dwelling
AGE	Proportion of owner-occupied units built prior to 1940
DIS	Weighted distances to five Boston employment centers
RAD	Index of accessibility to radial highways
TAX	Full-value property tax rate per $10,000
PTRATIO	Pupil-teacher ratio by town
B	$1000(Bk - 0.63)^2$ where Bk is the proportion of Black people by town
LSTAT	Percentage of lower status of the population
MEDV	Median value of owner-occupied homes in $1000s$

Methodology

Below is a detailed step-by-step case study for predicting Boston house prices using R. This case study will cover data loading, exploratory data analysis (EDA), data preprocessing, model building, evaluation, and visualization.

1. **Loading the Dataset**

```
# Load the necessary libraries
library(MASS)
# Load the Boston housing dataset
data(Boston)
```

2. **Exploratory Data Analysis (EDA)**

```
# Explore the structure of the dataset
str(Boston)
# Summary statistics of the dataset
summary(Boston)
# Visualize the distribution of the target variable (MEDV)
hist(Boston$medv, main = "Distribution of MEDV", xlab = "MEDV")
```

3. **Data Preprocessing**

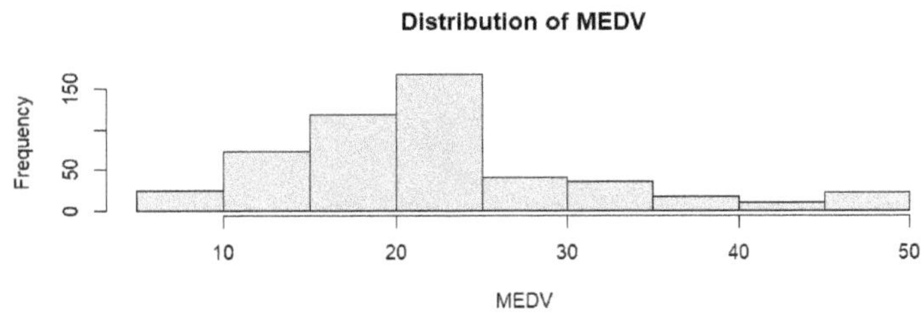

Figure 8.1: Histogram of the Boston Housing Dataset attributes.

```
# Check for missing values
colSums(is.na(Boston))

# Check for outliers
boxplot(Boston)

# Normalize/Standardize variables if necessary
# For example, using scale()
Boston_scaled <- as.data.frame(scale(Boston))
```

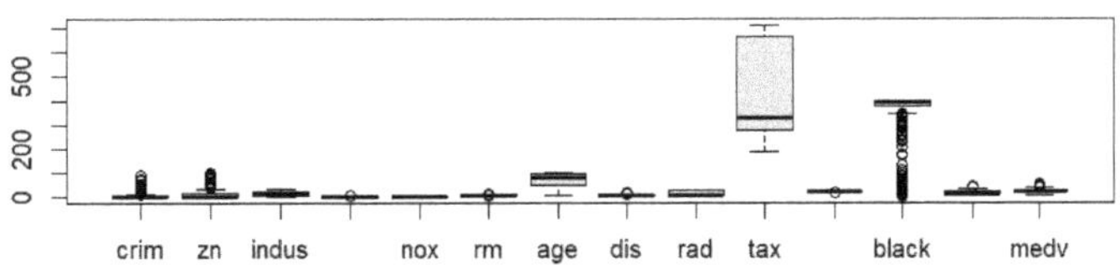

Figure 8.2: box plot of the Boston Housing Dataset attributes.

4. **Feature Selection**

```
# Correlation matrix
cor_matrix <- cor(Boston)
corrplot(cor_matrix, method = "color"
```

The resulting correlation matrix plot is shown below:

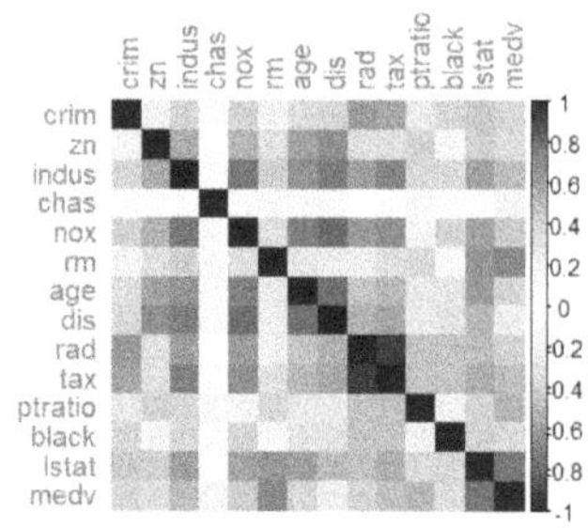

Figure 8.3: Correlation matrix plot of the Boston Housing Dataset attributes.

5. **Model Building (Linear Regression)**

```
# Build a linear regression model
model <- lm(medv ~ ., data = Boston)

# Model summary
summary(model)
```

6. **Model Evaluation**

```
# Predictions
predictions <- predict(model, newdata = Boston)

# Model evaluation metrics
library(Metrics)
mae <- mae(Boston$medv, predictions)
mse <- mse(Boston$medv, predictions)
rmse <- sqrt(mse)
r_squared <- r_squared(Boston$medv, predictions)
```

7. **Visualization**

```
# Scatterplot matrix
pairs(Boston)

# Residual plots
plot(model)

# Feature importance (if applicable)
# For example, with random forest model
library(randomForest)
rf_model <- randomForest(medv ~ ., data = Boston)
varImpPlot(rf_model)
```

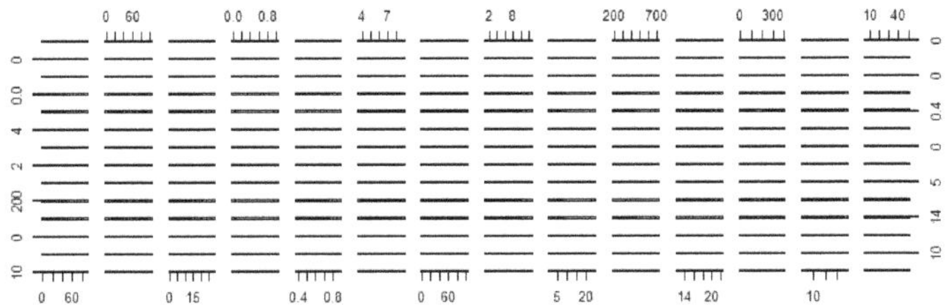

Figure 8.4: Scatterplot matrix

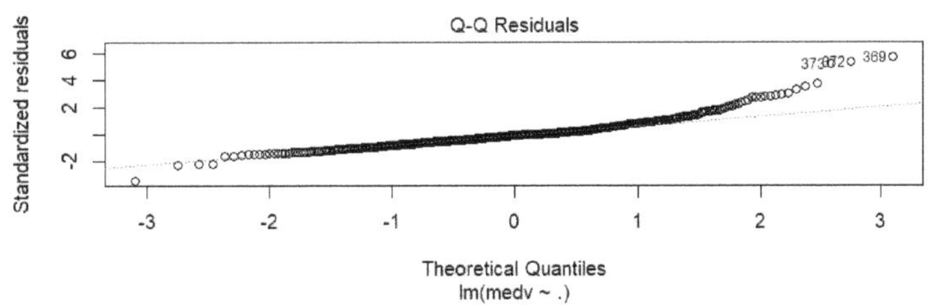

Figure 8.5: Residual plots

Conclusion

This case study outlines the process of predicting Boston house prices using R. By following these steps, one can load the dataset, explore its characteristics, preprocess the data, build regression models, evaluate their performance, and visualize the results. This comprehensive approach provides insights into the data and helps in developing accurate predictive models for real estate valuation.

Table 8.2: Boston House Price Prediction Using R (Page 1)

```
# Load the necessary libraries
library(MASS)
# Load the Boston housing dataset
data(Boston)

# Explore the structure of the dataset
str(Boston)

# Summary statistics of the dataset
summary(Boston)
# Visualize the distribution of the target variable (MEDV)
hist(Boston$medv, main = "Distribution of MEDV", xlab = "MEDV")

# Check for outliers
boxplot(Boston)

# Normalize/Standardize variables if necessary
# For example, using scale()
Boston_scaled <- as.data.frame(scale(Boston))

install.packages("corrplot")
library(corrplot)

# Correlation matrix
cor_matrix <- cor(Boston)
corrplot(cor_matrix, method = "color")

# Build a linear regression model
model <- lm(medv ~ ., data = Boston)
# Model summary
summary(model)

# Predictions
predictions <- predict(model, newdata = Boston)
# Model evaluation metrics

library(Metrics)
mae <- mae(Boston$medv, predictions)
mse <- mse(Boston$medv, predictions)
rmse <- sqrt(mse)
```

Table 8.3: Boston House Price Prediction Using R(Page 2)

```
      # Calculate R-squared
observed <- Boston$medv
predicted <- predictions
# Calculate mean of observed values
mean_observed <- mean(observed)

# Total sum of squares (TSS)
tss <- sum((observed - mean_observed)^2)

# Residual sum of squares (RSS)
rss <- sum((observed - predicted)^2)

# R-squared
r_squared <- 1 - (rss / tss)

print(mae)
print(mse)
print(rmse)
print(r_squared)


# Define the values of the predictors for the unknown instance

unknown_instance <- data.frame(
    crim = 0.03,
    zn = 0,
    indus = 2.95,
    chas = 0,
    nox = 0.4,
    rm = 6,
    age = 60,
    dis = 6,
    rad = 3,
    tax = 250,
    ptratio = 15,
    black = 330,
    lstat = 5
)

# Make predictions for the unknown instance
predicted_value <- predict(model, newdata = unknown_instance)
print(predicted_value)
```

8.2 Flower Power: Iris Study

Introduction The Iris dataset is a classic dataset in the field of machine learning and statistics. It consists of measurements of three different species of iris flowers: setosa, versicolor, and virginica. In this report, we will explore the Iris dataset and perform classification using R, a powerful programming language for statistical computing and graphics.

Dataset Overview The Iris dataset contains four features: sepal length, sepal width, petal length, and petal width. Each sample in the dataset is associated with one of the three species of iris flowers. Our objective is to build a classification model that can accurately predict the species of iris flowers based on these four features.

Methodology We will follow these steps to perform classification on the Iris dataset:

1. Data Loading and Exploration
   First, let's load the Iris dataset into R and explore its structure, summary statistics, and visualizations to gain insights into the data.

   ```
   # Load the Iris dataset
   data(iris)
   head(iris)  # Display the first few rows of the dataset
   summary(iris)  # Summary statistics of the dataset
   ```

   The provided R code loads the Iris dataset and displays the first few rows as well as summary statistics of the dataset.

2. Data Preprocessing

   Before building the classification model, we need to preprocess the data. This includes handling missing values, feature scaling, and splitting the dataset into training and testing sets.

   ```
   install.packages("ggplot2")
   # Visualization of the Iris dataset
   library(ggplot2)



   # Pairplot to visualize relationships between features
   pairs(iris[,1:4], main="Pairplot of Iris Dataset",
   pch=21, bg = c("red", "green3", "blue")[unclass(iris$Species)])
   ```

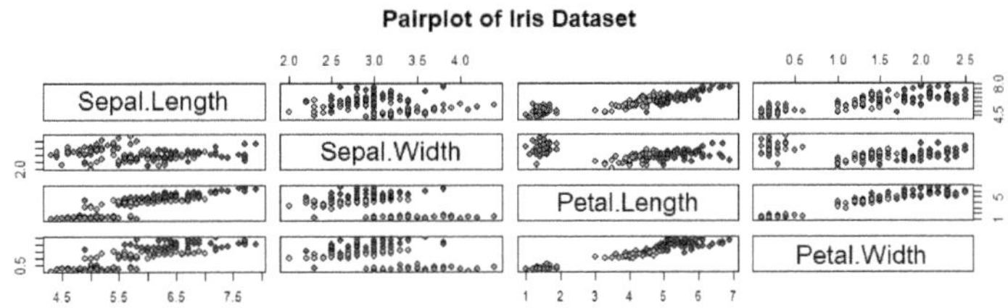

Figure 8.6: Pair Plot of iris Dataset.

```
# Boxplot to visualize distribution of features by species
ggplot(iris, aes(x = Species,
y = Sepal.Length, fill = Species)) +
  geom_boxplot() +
  labs(title = "Distribution of Sepal Length by Species")
```

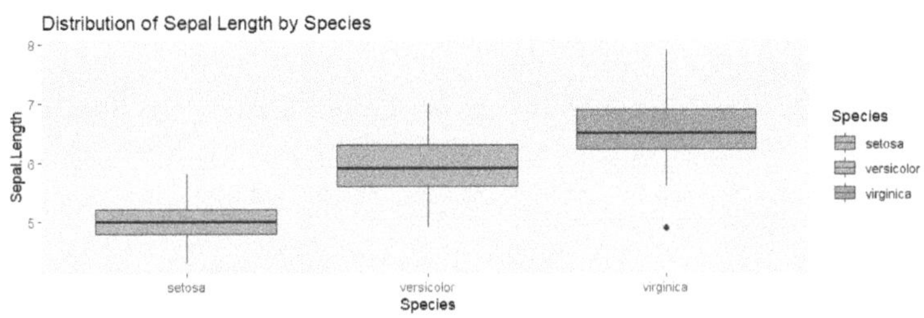

Figure 8.7: Distribution of Sepal Length By Species

```
ggplot(iris, aes(x = Species,
y = Sepal.Width, fill = Species)) +
  geom_boxplot() +
  labs(title = "Distribution of Sepal Width by Species")
```

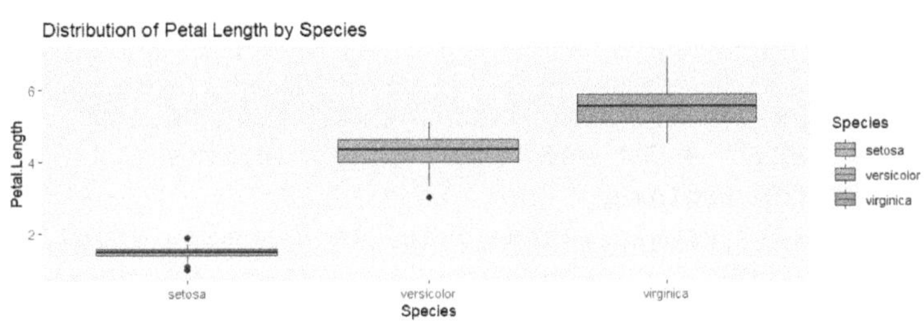

Figure 8.8: Distribution of Petal Length By Species.

```
ggplot(iris, aes(x = Species,
y = Petal.Length, fill = Species)) +
  geom_boxplot() +
  labs(title = "Distribution of Petal Length by Species")
```

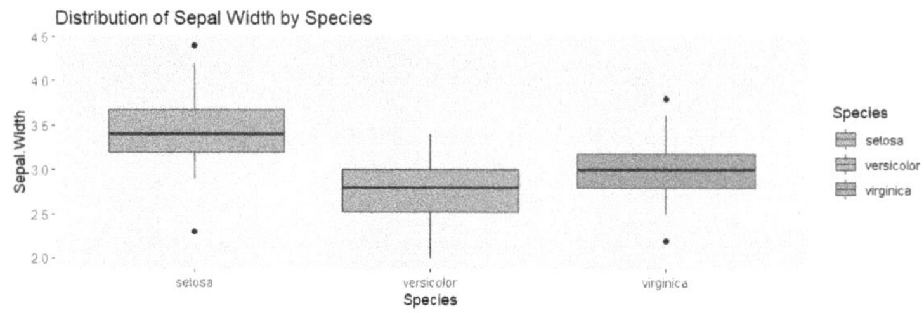

Figure 8.9: Distribution of Sepal Width By Species.

```
ggplot(iris, aes(x = Species,
y = Petal.Width, fill = Species)) +
  geom_boxplot() +
  labs(title = "Distribution of Petal Width by Species")
```

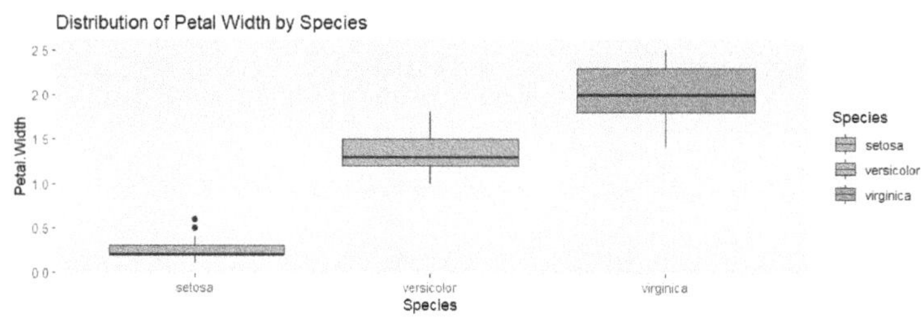

Figure 8.10: Distribution of Petal Width By Species.

```
# Check for missing values
sum(is.na(iris))

# Split the dataset into training and testing sets
set.seed(123)  # Set seed for reproducibility
   # 70% for training
trainIndex <- sample(1:nrow(iris), 0.7 * nrow(iris))

trainData <- iris[trainIndex, ]
testData <- iris[-trainIndex, ]
```

The data preprocessing steps involve checking for missing values and splitting the dataset into training and testing sets.

3. Model Training
   We will use a simple classification algorithm, such as logistic regression or k-nearest neighbors (KNN), to train our model.

```
    # Train the classification by KNN
library(class)
k <- 3  # Number of neighbors
predicted_knn <- knn(trainData[, -5], testData[, -5],
                          trainData[, 5], k)
```

   We train the classification model using logistic regression or K-nearest neighbors (KNN) algorithm.

4. Model Evaluation
   Now, we will evaluate the performance of our classification model using appropriate metrics such as accuracy, precision, recall, and F1-score.

```
# Evaluate the model


install.packages("caret")
library(caret)


# Compute confusion matrix
confusionMatrix(table(predicted_knn, testData$Species))
```

The following table shows the confusion matrix and overall statistics for the K-nearest neighbors (KNN) model:

	setosa	**versicolor**	**virginica**
setosa	14	0	0
versicolor	0	17	0
virginica	0	1	13

Table 8.4: Confusion Matrix

Overall Statistics:

- Accuracy: 0.9778
- 95% CI: (0.8823, 0.9994)

- No Information Rate: 0.4
- P-Value [Acc ¿ NIR]: $< 2.2 \times 10^{-16}$
- Kappa: 0.9664

Statistics by Class:

Table 8.5: Class-wise Statistics

Class	Setosa	Versicolor	Virginica
Sensitivity	1.0000	0.9444	1.0000
Specificity	1.0000	1.0000	0.9688
Pos Pred Value	1.0000	1.0000	0.9286
Neg Pred Value	1.0000	0.9643	1.0000
Prevalence	0.3111	0.4000	0.2889
Detection Rate	0.3111	0.3778	0.2889
Detection Prevalence	0.3111	0.3778	0.3111
Balanced Accuracy	1.0000	0.9722	0.9844

We evaluate the performance of the classification model K-nearest neighbors (KNN) .

5. Predicting Unknown Instance:

   We create a data frame representing the measurements of the unknown instance. Then, we use the trained K-nearest neighbors (KNN) to predict the species of the unknown instance. Finally, we print out the predicted species of KNN model

```
# Collect measurements of the unknown instance
unknown_instance <- data.frame(


  Sepal.Length = 5.1,
  Sepal.Width = 3.5,
  Petal.Length = 1.4,
  Petal.Width = 0.2


)

# For K-nearest neighbors (KNN)
predicted_species_knn <- knn(trainData[, -5],unknown_instance,
                             trainData[, 5],k)
print(predicted_species_knn)

[1] setosa
Levels: setosa versicolor virginica
```

Table 8.6: Classification of Iris Species using R(Page 1)

```
# Load the Iris dataset
data(iris)
head(iris) # Display the first few rows of the dataset
summary(iris) # Summary statistics of the dataset

# Install and load ggplot2 package for visualization
install.packages("ggplot2")
library(ggplot2)

# Pairplot to visualize relationships between features
pairs(iris[,1:4], main="Pairplot of Iris Dataset",
pch=21, bg = c("red", "green3", "blue")[unclass(iris$Species)])

# Boxplot to visualize distribution of features by species
ggplot(iris, aes(x = Species, y = Sepal.Length, fill = Species)) +
                     geom_boxplot() +
                     labs(title = "Distribution of Sepal Length by Species")

ggplot(iris, aes(x = Species, y = Sepal.Width, fill = Species)) +
                     geom_boxplot() +
                     labs(title = "Distribution of Sepal Width by Species")

ggplot(iris, aes(x = Species, y = Petal.Length, fill = Species)) +
                     geom_boxplot() +
                     labs(title = "Distribution of Petal Length by Species")

ggplot(iris, aes(x = Species, y = Petal.Width, fill = Species)) +
                     geom_boxplot() +
                     labs(title = "Distribution of Petal Width by Species")

# Check for missing values
sum(is.na(iris))
```

Table 8.7: Classification of Iris Species using R(Page 2)

```
# Split the dataset into training and testing sets
set.seed(123)  # Set seed for reproducibility

trainIndex <- sample(1:nrow(iris), 0.7 * nrow(iris))  # 70% for training
trainData <- iris[trainIndex, ]
testData <- iris[-trainIndex, ]

# Train the classification K-nearest neighbors (KNN) model
library(class)
k <- 3  # Number of neighbors
predicted_knn <- knn(trainData[, -5], testData[, -5], trainData[, 5], k)

# Install and load caret package for model evaluation
install.packages("caret")
library(caret)

# Compute confusion matrix
confusionMatrix(table(predicted_knn, testData$Species))

# Predict species of unknown instance using K-nearest neighbors (KNN)
unknown_instance <- data.frame(
  Sepal.Length = 5.1,
  Sepal.Width = 3.5,
  Petal.Length = 1.4,
  Petal.Width = 0.2
)

predicted_species_knn <- knn(trainData[,-5],unknown_instance,
                                         trainData[, 5], k)
print(predicted_species_knn)
```

8.3 Automobile Clustering Analysis

Introduction

Clustering analysis uncovers patterns by grouping similar data points. This case study applies K-means clustering to the mtcars dataset in R. With measurements from 1970s motor trend tests on 32 automobiles, it reveals insights into automotive features and their relationships.

Objective Apply K-means clustering to mtcars dataset in R to uncover hidden patterns and relationships among automotive features for analysis.

Dataset Overview The dataset was extracted from the 1974 Motor Trend US magazine and comprises fuel consumption and 10 aspects of automobile design and performance for 32 automobiles (1973-74 models). It is represented as a data frame with 32 observations on 11 numeric variables:

- `mpg`: Miles/(US) gallon
- `cyl`: Number of cylinders
- `disp`: Displacement (cu.in.)
- `hp`: Gross horsepower
- `drat`: Rear axle ratio
- `wt`: Weight (1000 lbs)
- `qsec`: 1/4 mile time
- `vs`: Engine (0 = V-shaped, 1 = straight)
- `am`: Transmission (0 = automatic, 1 = manual)
- `gear`: Number of forward gears
- `carb`: Number of carburetors

Clustering of mtcars Dataset using K-means
Load the Dataset

```
data(mtcars)
```

This line loads the mtcars dataset into the R environment.

Display the First Few Rows of the Dataset

```
head(mtcars)
```

```
                   mpg cyl disp  hp drat    wt  qsec vs am gear carb
Mazda RX4         21.0   6  160 110 3.90 2.620 16.46  0  1    4    4
Mazda RX4 Wag     21.0   6  160 110 3.90 2.875 17.02  0  1    4    4
Datsun 710        22.8   4  108  93 3.85 2.320 18.61  1  1    4    1
Hornet 4 Drive    21.4   6  258 110 3.08 3.215 19.44  1  0    3    1
Hornet Sportabout 18.7   8  360 175 3.15 3.440 17.02  0  0    3    2
Valiant           18.1   6  225 105 2.76 3.460 20.22  1  0    3    1
```

Figure 8.11: Few rows of the dataset

This command displays the first six rows of the mtcars dataset, providing a glimpse of its structure and content.

Perform Clustering using K-means Algorithm

```
set.seed(123) # Set seed for reproducibility
num_clusters <- 3 # Number of clusters
kmeans_model <- kmeans(mtcars, centers = num_clusters)
```

Sets the seed for reproducibility, ensuring that the results are consistent across different runs.

`set.seed(123)`

Specifies the number of clusters desired.

num$_{c}lusters < -3$

`kmeans_model <- kmeans(mtcars, centers = num_clusters)`

`View the Cluster Centers`

```
kmeans_model$centers
```

`This command displays the centroid coordinates of each cluster in the K-means model.`

```
       mpg      cyl     disp       hp     drat       wt     qsec        vs        am
1 17.01429 7.428571 276.0571 150.7143 2.994286 3.601429 18.11857 0.2857143 0.0000000
2 14.64444 8.000000 388.2222 232.1111 3.343333 4.161556 16.40444 0.0000000 0.2222222
3 24.50000 4.625000 122.2937  96.8750 4.002500 2.518000 18.54312 0.7500000 0.6875000
      gear     carb
1 3.000000 2.142857
2 3.444444 4.000000
3 4.125000 2.437500
```

Figure 8.12: cluster centers

`Add Cluster Labels to the Dataset`

```
mtcars$cluster <- as.factor(kmeans_model$cluster)
```

This line adds a new column called cluster to the mtcars dataset, containing the cluster labels assigned by the K-means algorithm.

Plot Clusters for Two Variables (mpg vs. wt)

```
plot(mpg ~ wt, data = mtcars, col = cluster, pch = 19,
     main = "Clustering of mtcars Dataset (mpg vs. wt)",
     xlab = "Weight (1000 lbs)", ylab = "Miles/(US) gallon")
```

This command creates a scatter plot of miles per gallon (mpg) against weight (wt) for the mtcars dataset. Data points are colored according to their assigned cluster, and cluster labels are represented by different symbols (pch).

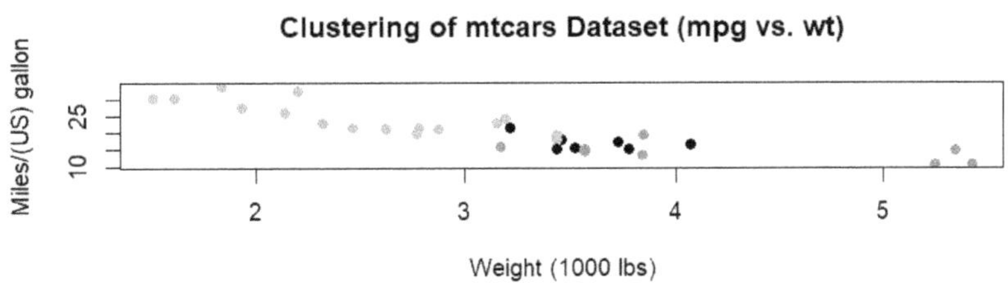

Figure 8.13: Clustering of mtcars dataset

Add Cluster Centers to the Plot

```
points(kmeans_model$centers[, c("wt", "mpg")],
col = 1:num_clusters, pch = 8, cex = 2)
```

Adds the cluster centers (centroid coordinates) to the scatter plot created in the previous step. Each cluster center is represented by a larger symbol (pch = 8) with a distinct color.

Add Legend to the Plot

```
legend("topright", legend = paste("Cluster", 1:num_clusters), col
= 1:num_clusters, pch = 19)
```

Adds a legend to the scatter plot, indicating the cluster labels and their corresponding colors.

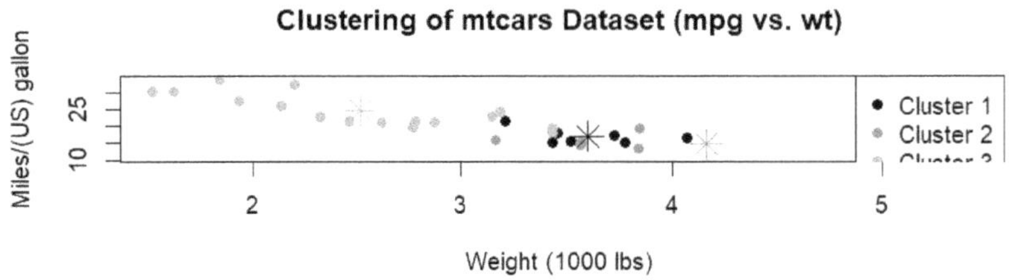

Figure 8.14: Clustering of mtcars Dataset with labeled Clusters

Table 8.8: Performing clustering on mtcars dataset using R

```
# Load the dataset
data(mtcars)

# Perform clustering using K-means algorithm
set.seed(123)  # Set seed for reproducibility
num_clusters <- 3  # Number of clusters
kmeans_model <- kmeans(mtcars, centers = num_clusters)

# View the cluster centers
kmeans_model$centers

# Add cluster labels to the dataset
mtcars$cluster <- as.factor(kmeans_model$cluster)

# Plot clusters for two variables, say mpg and wt
plot(mpg ~ wt, data = mtcars, col = cluster, pch = 19,
     main = "Clustering of mtcars Dataset (mpg vs. wt)",
     xlab = "Weight (1000 lbs)", ylab = "Miles/(US) gallon")

# Add cluster centers to the plot
points(kmeans_model$centers[, c("wt", "mpg")], col = 1:num_clusters,
                           pch = 8,cex = 2)
legend("topright", legend = paste("Cluster", 1:num_clusters),
col = 1:num_clusters, pch = 19)
```

Appendix A

Answers

Fill in the blanks

Chapter-1

1. dimensionality reduction
2. scaling
3. basis
4. determinant
5. hyperplane
6. variables
7. scalar
8. Pythagorean theorem
9. singular vectors and singular values
10. transformation

Chapter-2

1. outcomes
2. discrete
3. sample
4. null hypotheses
5. rejected
6. association
7. rejection region
8. normal
9. population parameters
10. sample means

Chapter-3

1. Predicting continuous outcomes
2. The relationship between variables is linear
3. $y = mx + b$
4. Relationships between multiple independent variables and one dependent variable
5. Continuous outcomes, categorical outcomes
6. $[0, 1]$
7. Probability
8. Independent variables
9. Perfect correlation
10. Heteroscedasticity

Chapter-4

1. data type
2. "package name"
3. comparison
4. table
5. (parameters)
6. iterative
7. errors
8. uniform
9. margins
10. multiple

Chapter-5

1. binary
2. instance-based
3. variance
4. over time
5. nodes or individuals
6. RMySQL
7. NoSQL
8. actual
9. clustering
10. values

Chapter-6

1. itemsets
2. statistical independence
3. consequent
4. dataset
5. reliability

MCQ Answers

Chapter-1

1. B) The study of collecting and analyzing data to gain insights
2. C) Linear Algebra
3. B) To model relationships between variables
4. B) A plane that divides a space into two half-spaces
5. C) Half space
6. A) They represent the magnitude of eigenvectors
7. A) Vectors that don't change direction when a linear transformation is applied
8. B) Using the Pythagorean theorem
9. C) Transposition
10. C) The number of non-zero rows after row reduction
11. B) Determining if a matrix is invertible
12. C) Rectangular matrix
13. A) To reduce the dimensionality of data
14. C) It decomposes a matrix into singular vectors and singular values
15. D) Data fabrication
16. B) To penalize large coefficients in the model
17. B) Variance
18. A) |A| × |B| cos()
19. A) Gradient Descent
20. A) To offset the influence of independent variables

Chapter-2

1. B) A variable whose outcome is determined by chance
2. C) A function that describes the probability distribution of discrete random variables

3. B) A function that describes the probability distribution of discrete random variables
4. C) The likelihood of observing a specific value of a continuous random variable
5. C) Mean
6. C) The middle value of a sorted dataset
7. B) To disprove a hypothesis
8. B) A hypothesis that is assumed to be true
9. A) The probability of rejecting the null hypothesis when it is true
10. A) Rejecting the null hypothesis when it is true
11. A) Accepting the null hypothesis when it is true
12. C) Independent samples t-test
13. C) To test for association between categorical variables
14. A) The difference between observed and expected frequencies
15. A) The value of the test statistic that determines the rejection region
16. C) Analysis of Variance (ANOVA)
17. A) The distribution of data is normal
18. B) Confidence intervals
19. C) The standard deviation of the distribution of sample means
20. C) The standard deviation of the distribution of sample means

Chapter-3

1. B) Predicting continuous outcomes
2. A) The relationship between variables is linear
3. A) y = mx + b
4. A) To model relationships between multiple independent variables and one dependent variable
5. A) Linear regression predicts continuous outcomes, while logistic regression predicts categorical outcomes

6. B) [0, 1]
7. C) To transform the linear combination of predictors into a probability
8. A) The proportion of variance in the dependent variable explained by the independent variable
9. A) A situation where there is perfect correlation between the independent variables
10. C) To check for linearity of the relationship
11. B) A situation where the residuals have a non-constant variance across different values of the independent variable
12. C) Ridge regression
13. B) To standardize the range of values of independent variables
14. B) The significance of the coefficient
15. A) log(p)
16. D) Independence of observations
17. C) Area Under the ROC Curve (AUC)
18. B) To reduce overfitting
19. C) Logistic regression

Chapter-4

1. B) Data analysis and statistical computing
2. A) install.packages("package name")
3. A) Concatenation
4. C) Creates a data frame
5. A) Returns the storage mode of an object
6. A) ^
7. B) To perform comparisons
8. C) function name ¡- function(parameters)
9. C) for loop
10. B) Steps through the code line by line for debugging

11. C) rnorm()
12. C) ? function name
13. D) $
14. A) Applies a function over margins of an array
15. A) as.character()
16. B) an. omit()
17. A) To create a subset of data based on a condition
18. B) To merge two or more data frames
19. B) matrix()

Chapter-5

1. C) Accuracy
2. A) Sigmoid function
3. B) Calculates the distance between data points
4. B) KNN works well with high-dimensional data
5. C) To minimize the variance within clusters
6. D) Update cluster centroids based on the mean of data points
7. A) To predict future events based on historical data
8. B) PageRank algorithm
9. C) Using readSQL() function
10. C) MongoDB
11. B) Metrics used to evaluate the accuracy of classification models
12. B) glm()
13. C) Majority vote of nearest neighbors
14. A) kmeans()
15. C) Observations are recorded at regular intervals
16. B) Betweenness centrality
17. C) Using readMongo() function
18. B) Sentiment analysis

19. B) To divide data points into distinct clusters

Chapter-6

1. A) A technique for finding patterns in data
2. B) It is a principle that states that a subset of a frequent itemset must also be frequent.
3. B) Frequent itemsets are the input to association rule mining, while association rules are the output.
4. C) It evaluates the strength of association between antecedent and consequent, compared to statistical independence.
5. C) Measures used to quantify the significance and reliability of discovered rules.
6. C) Apriori
7. B) The frequency of occurrence of an itemset in the dataset.
8. B) It requires multiple passes over the dataset.
9. B) The difference between observed and expected frequencies of an itemset.
10. B) Confidence